Summer Bridge Activities™

creation and design
Michele D. Van Leeuwen

exercise illustrations by
Amanda Sorensen

Third Grade to Fourth Grade

written by
Julia Ann Hobbs
Carla Dawn Fisher

Summer Bridge Activities™ Contains...

Fun, skill-based activities in **reading, writing, arithmetic,** and **language arts** with additional activities in **geography** and **science** to keep your child busy, happy, and learning! SBA is divided into three sections for review and preview with pages numbered by day. Children complete their work quickly with the easy-to-use format, leaving lots of time for play!

A **Reading Book List** based on the Accelerated Reader Program.

Incentive Contracts to encourage summer learning and reward your child's efforts. **"Discover Something New"** lists of creative things to do are found on the back of each SBA Incentive Contract Calendar for when your child says the inevitable: "What can I do? I'm bored."

Comprehensive **Word Lists,** which contain words to sound, read, and spell, challenge children and encourage them to build their vocabulary. SBA 3–4 also contains **Division and Multiplication Flashcards, 0–10.**

Tear-out answer pages to help correct your child's work.

An official **Certificate of Completion** to be awarded for successfully completing the workbook.

Mr. Fredrickson

Ms. Hansen

Here are some groups who think our books are great!

SBA
YOUTH EDUCATION EXCELLENCE
1993-99

HBP EDUCATION EXCELLENCE 1995 APPROVED

PARENTS' CHOICE APPROVED

Hey Kids and Parents!
Log on to www.summerbrains.com
for more eye-boggling, mind-bending, brain-twisting summer fun...
It's where summerbrains
like you hang out!
www.summerbrains.com

Summer Bridge Activities™
3rd to 4th Grade

For information, write
Rainbow Bridge Publishing, Inc.
PO Box 571470
Salt Lake City, Utah 84157-1470
801/268-8887
www.summerbridgeactivities.com

Publisher
Scott G. Van Leeuwen

Associate Publisher
George Starks

Series Creator
Michele D. Van Leeuwen

Product Development Director
Dante J. Orazzi

Editorial Director
Paul Rawlins

Copy Editors and Proofreaders
Kathleen Bratcher, Jerold Johnson, Debra Reed,
Kersten Swinyard, and Jennifer Willes

Additional Content
Clareen Arnold, Molly McMahon

Graphic Design and Layout
Andy Carlson, Robyn Funk, Zack Johnson, and Amanda Sorensen

Please visit our website at
www.summerbridgeactivities.com
for supplements, additions, and corrections to this book.

Ninth Edition 2003

For orders call 1-800-598-1441
Discounts available for quantity orders

ISBN: 1-887923-06-3

PRINTED IN THE UNITED STATES OF AMERICA
10 9

Table of Contents

Dear Parents,

Thank you for choosing Summer Bridge Activities™ to help reinforce your child's classroom skills while away from school. This year, I am proud to offer you this special edition, "Building Better Bodies and Behavior," to help your children develop not only their minds this summer, but their bodies and character as well. I hope you enjoy!

Your personal involvement is so important to your child's immediate and long-term academic success. No matter how wonderful your child's classroom experience is, your involvement outside the classroom will make it that much better!

I originally created Summer Bridge Activities™ because as a parent of a first grader, summer was quickly approaching and I was concerned that the skills he had worked so hard to develop would be forgotten. I was apprehensive about his adjustment to school after three months of play and wanted to help in any way I could. I spoke with his teacher, other school administrators, and parents and found I was not alone in my concerns. I was told by several educators that up to 80% of what children are taught in school can be lost, unless that knowledge is reinforced quickly and continuously! I certainly did not want this to happen to my son!

I looked for appropriate workbooks but could not find any that compared with the Department of Education curriculum guidelines and included all the basic skills in an easy-to-use format. So, as a concerned parent, I organized a team of award-winning teachers and informed educators to create a series of workbooks that would make reviewing classroom skills—including reading, writing, arithmetic, geography, and language arts—fun and rewarding. The end result was the Summer Bridge Activities™ workbook that you have in your hands right now! I am confident that you will enjoy using it with your child.

Thanks again for choosing this wonderful program to assist with your child's academic success. I wish you the best of luck in helping your child get the most out of his/her education. Also, we at RBP welcome you to **www.summerbrains.com** where you will find additional fun, interactive learning games, ideas, and activities for you and your child at no additional cost. We look forward to seeing you there! Have a great summer and happy learning!

Sincerely,

Michele D. Van Leeuwen
Creator of Summer Bridge Activities™

Inside Summer Bridge Activities™

Ms. Hansen takes you INSIDE

The exercises found in Summer Bridge Activities™ (SBA) are easy to understand and are presented in a way that allows your child to review familiar skills and then be progressively challenged on more difficult subjects. In addition to academic exercises, SBA contains many other activities to challenge and reinforce reading comprehension, phonemic awareness, and letter, word, and number recognition.

Sections of Summer Bridge Activities™

☆ There are three sections in Summer Bridge Activities™, the first and second sections review, the third previews.

☆ Each section begins with an SBA Incentive Contract Calendar.

☆ Each day your child will complete an activity in reading, writing, arithmetic, and language skills. The activities progressively become more challenging.

☆ Each page is numbered by day.

☆ Your child will need a pencil, ruler, eraser, and crayons to complete the activities.

Books Children Love to Read

SBA contains a Reading Book List with a variety of titles, including many that are found in the Accelerated Reader Program.

RBP recommends that parents read to their pre-kindergarten and kindergarten–1st grade children 5–10 minutes each day and then ask questions about the story to reinforce comprehension. For higher grade levels, RBP recommends the following daily reading times: grades 1–2, 10–20 minutes; grades 2–3, 20–30 minutes; grades 3–4, 30–45 minutes; grades 4–5 and 5–6, 45–60 minutes.

It is important that the parent and child decide an amount of reading time and write it on the SBA Incentive Contract Calendar.

SBA Incentive Contract Calendars

Calendars are located at the beginning of each section.

We suggest that the parent and child sign the SBA Incentive Contract Calendar before the child begins each section.

When your child completes one day of Summer Bridge Activities™, he/she may color or initial the pencil.

Refer to the recommended reading times. When your child completes the agreed reading time each day, he/she may color or initial the book.

The parent may initial the SBA Incentive Contract Calendar once the activities have been completed.

Let your child explore and experiment with the "Discover Something New" activities found on the back of each SBA Incentive Contract Calendar.

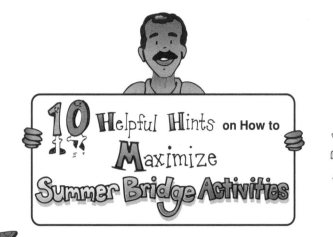

10 Helpful Hints on How to Maximize Summer Bridge Activities

1 First, let your child explore the book. Flip through the pages and look at the activities with your child to help him/her become familiar with the book.

2 Help select a good time for reading or working on the activities. Suggest a time before your child has played outside and becomes too tired to do the work.

3 Provide any necessary materials. A pencil, ruler, eraser, and crayons are all that are required.

4 Offer positive guidance. Children need a great deal of guidance. Remember, the activities are not meant to be tests. You want to create a relaxed and positive attitude toward learning. Work through at least one example on each page with your child. "Think aloud" and show your child how to solve problems.

5 Give your child plenty of time to think. You may be surprised by how much children can do on their own.

6 Stretch your child's thinking beyond the page. If you are reading a storybook, you might ask, "What do you think will happen next?" or "What would you do if this happened to you?" Encourage your child to name objects that begin with certain letters or count the number of items in your shopping cart. Also, children often enjoy making up their own stories with illustrations.

7 Reread stories and occasionally flip through completed pages. Completed pages and books will be a source of pride to your child and will help show how much he/she accomplished over the summer.

8 Read and work on activities while outside. Take the workbook out in the backyard, to the park, or to a family camp out. It can be fun wherever you are!

9 Encourage siblings, babysitters, and neighborhood children to help with reading and activities. Other children are often perfect for providing the one-on-one attention necessary to reinforce reading skills.

10 Give plenty of approval! Stickers and stamps, or even a hand-drawn funny face, are effective for recognizing a job well done. When your child completes the book, hang his/her Certificate of Completion where everyone can see it. At the end of the summer, your child can feel proud of his/her accomplishments and will be eager for school to start.

words to
SOUND, READ,
and S-P-E-L-L

At the end of each section are words to sound out, read, and spell.

Together you and your child can...

Write your favorite words on flashcards. Make two sets and play the matching game (in order to keep the two matching cards, you have to know their meaning or spelling).

Draw pictures of exciting words.

Use as many words as you can from the list to make up five questions, statements, or explanations.

Write a story using as many words as you can from the word list.

Write a list of words you find while traveling to the grocery store, on vacation, or on the way to a friend's house.

Write a list of colors.

Write a list of words you have a hard time spelling.

Write a list of action verbs.

Practice writing each word five times.

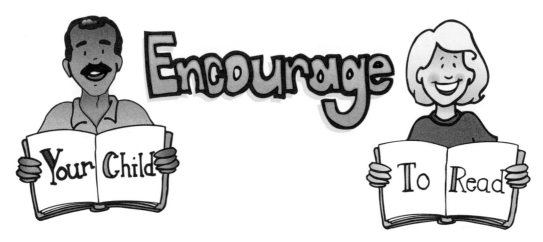

Reading is the primary means to all learning. If a child cannot read effectively, other classroom subjects can remain out of reach.

You were probably the first person to introduce your child to the wonderful world of reading. As your child grows, it is important to continue encouraging his/her interest in reading to support the skills being taught in school.

This summer, make reading a priority in your household. Set aside time each day to read aloud to your child at bedtime or after lunch or dinner. Encourage your child take a break from playing and stretch out with a book found on the Summer Bridge Activities™ Reading Book List. Choose a title that you have never read, or introduce your child to some of the books you enjoyed when you were his or her age! Books only seem to get better with time!

Visit the library to find books that meet your child's specific interests. Ask a librarian which books are popular among children of your child's grade. Take advantage of summer storytelling activities at the library. Ask the librarian about other resources such as stories on cassette, compact disc, and the Internet.

Encourage reading in all settings and daily activities. Encourage your child to read house numbers, street signs, window banners, and packaging labels. Encourage your child to tell stories using pictures.

Best of all, show your child how much YOU like to read! Sit down with your child when he/she reads and enjoy a good book yourself. After dinner, share stories and ideas from newspapers and magazines that might interest your child. Make reading a way of life this summer!

Reading Book List

Adler, David
    Cam Jansen: And the Mystery of the Television Dog

Ackerman, Karen
    The Night Crossing

Barrett, Judi
    Cloudy with a Chance of Meatballs

Berenstain, Stan and Jan
    Berenstain Bears—chapter books
      Accept No Substitutes
      At Camp Crush
      And the Dress Code
      And the Drug Free Zone
      And the Galloping Ghost
      Ant the Giddy Grandma
      Gotta Dance
      Media Madness

Blume, Judy
    Freckle Juice

Brown, Jeff
    Flat Stanley

Burton, Virginia Lee
    Katy and the Big Snow

Catling, Patrick Skene
    Chocolate Touch

Cherry, Lynne
    Great Kapok Tree: A Tale of the Amazon Rain
      Forest

Christian, Mary Blount
    Sebastian (Super Sleuth) and the Copycat Crime

Cleary, Beverly
    Ramona Quimby: Age 8
    Muggie Maggie

Clifford, Eth
    Flatfoot Fox and the Case of the Missing Whoooo

Cole, Joanna
    Magic School Bus: At the Water Works
    Magic School Bus: Inside the Earth
    Magic School Bus: On the Ocean Floor

Cooney, Barbara
    Miss Rumphius

Dalgliesh, Alice
    Courage of Sarah Noble

Danziger, Paula
    There's a Bat in Bunk Five
    Amber Brown Is Not a Crayon
    Amber Brown Goes Forth

DePaola, Tomie
    Legend of the Bluebonnet

Donnelly, Judy
    Wall of Names: Story of the Vietnam
      Veterans Memorial
    Who Shot the President? The Death of
      John F. Kennedy
    Moonwalk: First Trip to the Moon

Dorros, Arthur
    Abuela

Ernst, Lisa Campbell
    Nattie Parson's Good Luck Lamb

Fox, Paula
    Maurice's Room

Gardiner, John
    Stone Fox

Gleiter, Jan
    Paul Revere

Graff, Stewart
    Helen Keller: Toward the Light

Gutelle, Andrew
    Baseball's Best: Five True Stories

Havill, Juanita
    Treasure Nap

Hidaka, Masako
    Girl from the Snow Country

Demuth, Patricia Brennan
    In Trouble with Teacher

Jeschke, Susan
Perfect the Pig

Jonas, Ann
Aardvarks, Disembark!

Jukes, Mavis
Blackberries in the Dark

Kellogg, Steven
Paul Bunyan

Konigsburg, E. L.
The View from Saturday

Korman, Gordon
No Coins, Please

Krensky, Stephen
Witch Hunt

Kroll, Steven
Andrew Wants a Dog

Landon, Lucinda
Meg Macintosh and the Case of the Curious
Whale Watch

Lindgren, Astrid
Pippi Goes on Board

Little, Emily
Trojan Horse: How the Greeks
Won the War

Lobel, Arnold
Grasshopper on the Road
Book of Pigericks

Manes, Stephen
Be a Perfect Person in Just Three Days

McCloskey, Robert
Homer Price

McMullan, Kate
Dinosaur Hunters

O'Connor, Jim
Jackie Robinson and the Story
of All-Black Baseball

Osborne, Mary Pope
Moonhorse

Peet, Bill
Spooky Tail of Prewitt Peacock
Wump World

Pretulsky, Jack
The New Kid on the Block
Tyrannosaurus Was a Beast
Random House Book of Poetry for Children
(Selected by Jack Pretulsky)

Raskin, Ellen
Nothing Ever Happens on My Block

Rowling, J. K.
Harry Potter Series

Schroeder, Alan
A Story of Young Harriet Tubman

Sharmat, Marjorie Weinman
Nate the Great series

Smith, Janet Lee
The Monster in the Third Dresser Drawer
It's Not Easy Being George

Smith, Robert Kimmer
Chocolate Fever

Sobol, Donald J.
Encyclopedia Brown series

Stadler, John
Animal Cafe

Steig, William
The Amazing Bone
Sylvester and the Magic Pebble

Stock, Catherine
Emma's Dragon Hunt

Stoutenburg, Adrien
American Tall Tales

Waber, Bernard
Lyle, Lyle, Crocodile

Walter, Mildred Pitts
Justin and the Best Biscuits in the World

Whelan, Gloria
Next Spring an Oriole

White, E.B.
Charlotte's Web

Summer Bridge Activities™
Incentive Contract Calendar

Month _____

My parents and I decided that if I complete 15 days of
Summer Bridge Activities™ and read _____ minutes a day,
my incentive/reward will be:

_____

Child's Signature _____
Parent's Signature _____

Day 1   📖 ⭐ _____   Day 8   📖 ⭐ _____

Day 2   📖 ⭐ _____   Day 9   📖 ⭐ _____

Day 3   📖 ⭐ _____   Day 10   📖 ⭐ _____

Day 4   📖 ⭐ _____   Day 11   📖 ⭐ _____

Day 5   📖 ⭐ _____   Day 12   📖 ⭐ _____

Day 6   📖 ⭐ _____   Day 13   📖 ⭐ _____

Day 7   📖 ⭐ _____   Day 14   📖 ⭐ _____

                                      Day 15   📖 ⭐ _____

Child: Color the ⭐ for daily activities completed.
Color the 📖 for daily reading completed.

Parent: Initial the _____ for daily activities and reading
your child completes.

Discover Something New!

Fun Activity Ideas to Go Along with the First Section!

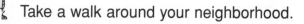

1. Set goals for your summer and post them on your refrigerator—plan fun rewards.

2. Sign up for a summer reading program at your library.

3. Plan a treasure hunt. Have older kids write clues for younger kids and make fun treasures.

4. Take a walk around your neighborhood.

5. Make up a "Bored List" of things to do.

6. Look at the weather map in the newspaper and check temperatures in other cities.

7. Play charades or another guessing game.

8. Plan a special activity for Father's Day with your dad, a special relative, or a friend.

9. Draw a map of your neighborhood on graph paper. Chart a walk.

10. Play a game that has been put away in your closet and forgotten about.

11. Plan a reading picnic in the backyard, park, or canyon.

12. Find a map of the U.S.—then map out your dream vacation.

13. Make a graph of the number of days the temperature rises over 90 degrees.

14. Find a colony of ants. Spill some food and see what happens.

15. Visit a grocery store and select a "mystery" food you've never tried, like kumquats.

Warm-up Addition and Subtraction Problems.
Remember: The answers to addition problems are called sums, while the answers to subtraction problems are called differences.

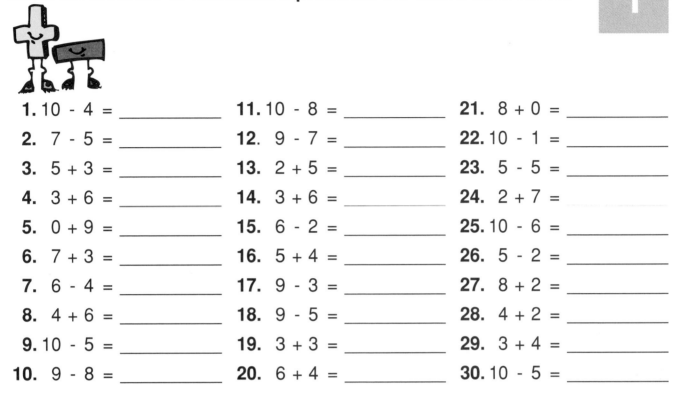

1. 10 - 4 = _____
2. 7 - 5 = _____
3. 5 + 3 = _____
4. 3 + 6 = _____
5. 0 + 9 = _____
6. 7 + 3 = _____
7. 6 - 4 = _____
8. 4 + 6 = _____
9. 10 - 5 = _____
10. 9 - 8 = _____

11. 10 - 8 = _____
12. 9 - 7 = _____
13. 2 + 5 = _____
14. 3 + 6 = _____
15. 6 - 2 = _____
16. 5 + 4 = _____
17. 9 - 3 = _____
18. 9 - 5 = _____
19. 3 + 3 = _____
20. 6 + 4 = _____

21. 8 + 0 = _____
22. 10 - 1 = _____
23. 5 - 5 = _____
24. 2 + 7 =
25. 10 - 6 = _____
26. 5 - 2 = _____
27. 8 + 2 = _____
28. 4 + 2 = _____
29. 3 + 4 = _____
30. 10 - 5 = _____

Practice writing the letters of the alphabet in cursive.

A   B   C   D   E   F   G

H   I   J   K   L   M   N

O   P   Q   R   S   T   U

V   W   X   Y   Z

a   b   c   d   e   f   g

h   i   j   k   l   m   n

o   p   q   r   s   t   u

v   w   x   y   z

Homonyms are words that sound the same but have different meanings. Write the correct word to complete the sentence.

threw
through
Their
They're
There
read
Red
two
to
too
paws
pause
flew
flu

1. I have _____ more days of school.
2. Have you _____ this book before?
3. _____ are ninety boxes left to open.
4. That lion has large _____.
5. We walked _____ the tall grass very quickly.
6. Would you please push _____ on the tape player?
7. The boys had _____ much work to do before dark.
8. _____ going on vacation next week.
9. My sister and I had the _____ last month.
10. Toby _____ the ball against the building all recess.
11. _____ is my favorite color.
12. _____ cousins are coming to stay for the summer.
13. We are going _____ Lake Louise this summer.
14. Hundreds of bats _____ out of the cave.

1. Put an X on all the odd numbers.
2. Circle all the capital letters.
3. Put a square around the greatest number.
4. Underline in order the numbers you use to count by twos to 40.
5. Put a triangle around the number that is four less than 62.
6. Write the capital letters you circled in order: _____

b	r	q	e	o	S	c	r	y	10	6	3
U	y	10	5	2	4	M	z	1	q	a	i
6	v	0	7	8	M	p	2	10	17	12	l
r	b	14	18	b	e	16	f	h	19	E	s
18	5	14	7	2	p	m	n	z	58	20	s
94	86	22	2	R	17	l	0	24	n	x	c
26	39	3	a	d	e	28	g	h	52	19	30
7	j	F	k	32	y	34	4	31	t	10	36
0	n	e	n	38	o	80	99	U	47	x	p
w	m	m	11	N	3	14	100	c	r	e	t
q	u	v	9	7	6	w	5	40	w	13	l

Fact Families.

EXAMPLE:

$\binom{9 \; 10}{1}$

| 9 | + | 1 | = | 10 | | 10 | - | 1 | = | 9 |
| 1 | + | 9 | = | 10 | | 10 | - | 9 | = | 1 |

Make fact families. Use the numbers in the circles.

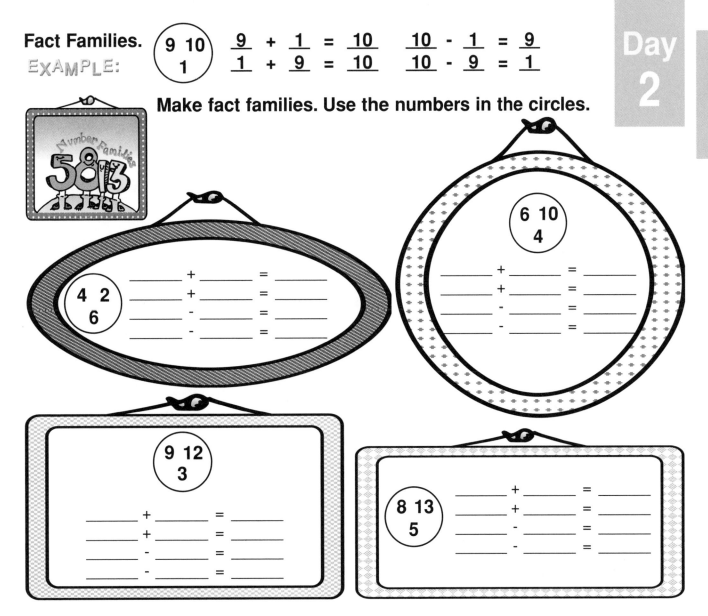

Practice writing these letters in cursive.

aaa   ccc   eee   üü

mmm   nnn   ooo

sss   rrr   wvw

xxx   wvwvw   uuuu

lll   ttt   bbb   ddd

kkk   fff   hhh

Read the story; then number the sentences in the order they happened.

Every summer my father wants to go on the same old trip that we have gone on for years. First, we pack the car full of everything we think we will need. We don't use most of it! Then, we drive all night to get to Camp Busy Bee where Dad camped when he was a boy. After we get settled, everyone has to go swimming in Cool Pool. The next day we hike. On the third day, we do crafts. Last year, I made a nutcracker. It broke before I got home. On the fourth day we go home (thank goodness).

_____ On the third day we do crafts.

_____ We drive all night.

_____ On the fourth day we go home.

_____ We pack the car.

_____ We go swimming in Cool Pool.

Study these often misspelled words. Write them in cursive two times; then have someone read them to you while you write them.

Now write them without looking.

1. their	_their_	_their_	**1.**	_____
2. there	_____	_____	**2.**	_____
3. until	_____	_____	**3.**	_____
4. to	_____	_____	**4.**	_____
5. too	_____	_____	**5.**	_____
6. two	_____	_____	**6.**	_____
7. unusual	_____	_____	**7.**	_____
8. touch	_____	_____	**8.**	_____
9. toe	_____	_____	**9.**	_____
10. tear	_____	_____	**10.**	_____
11. think	_____	_____	**11.**	_____
12. teeth	_____	_____	**12.**	_____

Sums and Differences through Eighteen.

14 − 9	13 − 5	9 + 8	9 + 9	15 − 8	11 − 7	16 − 8	12 + 3
7 + 5	8 + 8	12 − 6	15 + 3	18 − 9	5 + 6	12 − 7	11 + 6
18 − 9	4 + 8	11 − 4	15 − 9	13 − 8	14 − 6	7 + 9	17 − 8

Write these sentences correctly. Use capital letters and the right punctuation. Write them in cursive.

1. our class went on a field trip to the zoo

_____

_ _

2. did you like the giraffe or the bear best

_____

_ _

3. we met a snake called sneak

_____

_ _

4. how long did martha stay at the zoo

_____

_ _

5. her mother picked her up at three o'clock

_____

_ _

Suffixes come at the end of root, or base, words.
Finish these sentences by adding -less or -ful to the base word.

1. It was <u>thought</u>_____ of Jim to bring ice cream to the picnic.

2. Mark was <u>hope</u>_____ that he would get a part in the school play.

3. Baby puppies are <u>help</u>_____ for a few weeks.

4. Many snakes are <u>harm</u>_____ and will not hurt you.

5. We were very <u>care</u>_____ when we crossed the river on the log.

6. I feel bad when I see <u>home</u>_____ people.

7. That tool has been very <u>use</u>_____ to us.

8. We had a <u>fright</u>_____ experience on our vacation.

9. The children have been <u>help</u>_____ in our garden.

10. My grandfather seems <u>age</u>_____.

11. That old dog is <u>tooth</u>_____.

12. We are all <u>thank</u>_____ that our car did not crash.

Make a "Things that you might…" list of words for each category. These words will come in handy when you are writing stories.

<u>See</u>

<u>Hear</u>

<u>Smell</u>

<u>Touch</u>

<u>Taste</u>

Read and think. Write the problem to show how you got your answer.

EXAMPLE: John has 18 birds. His cousin, Jim, has 9. How many more birds does John have than Jim?

<u>18</u> - <u>9</u> = <u>9</u> birds

3. My family and I will go to the beach in July. We go every year. Last year, my sister found 9 shells, my brother found 5, and I only found 4. How many shells did we find? Write the problem.

_____

1. Carla went on a weekend trip. She took 16 pictures. Only 8 pictures turned out. How many did not turn out?

____ ◯ ____ = ____ pictures

4. Dixie worked for her uncle last summer. She made $16 the first two weeks. She spent $5 to go swimming. How much did she have left? Write the problem.

_____

2. In June, I read 6 books, in July, 3, and in August, 7. How many books did I read this summer?

___ ◯ ___ ◯ ___ = ___ books

5. In the pond, Sue counted 14 fish and 9 tadpoles. How many fewer tadpoles are there than fish? Write the problem.

_____

Is it a complete sentence? <u>Remember</u>**: A sentence is a group of words that tell a complete idea. Write <u>yes</u> for complete sentences. Write <u>no</u> if it is not a complete sentence.**

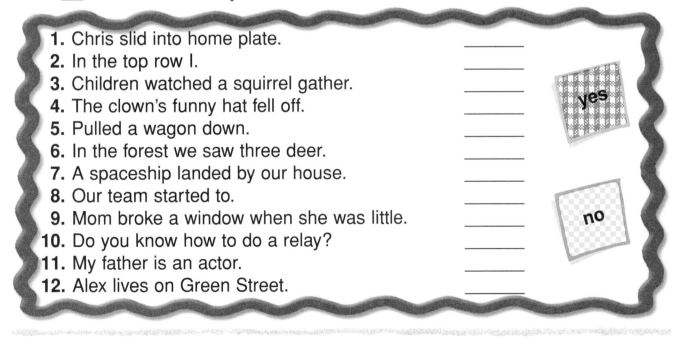

1. Chris slid into home plate. _____
2. In the top row I. _____
3. Children watched a squirrel gather. _____
4. The clown's funny hat fell off. _____
5. Pulled a wagon down. _____
6. In the forest we saw three deer. _____
7. A spaceship landed by our house. _____
8. Our team started to. _____
9. Mom broke a window when she was little. _____
10. Do you know how to do a relay? _____
11. My father is an actor. _____
12. Alex lives on Green Street. _____

yes

no

Prefixes: Read this story, using what you know about the prefixes: dis-, in-, re-, un-. The first one has been done for you.

My Uncle Paul works in a bookstore. Uncle Paul always helped me find the books I needed. He was never **dis** pleased if I asked for his help. I _____call the day I asked for a book about unsolved mysteries. Uncle Paul _____covered some on the very top of the back shelf. They were dirty and smelled dusty. They looked as if they had been _____touched for years. I started reading one about a phantom. As I looked _____side, I noticed that some pages were missing. They were the pages at the very end of the book. "Gadzooks and rats!" I said. "This story is _____complete. Now I'll never know who the phantom is." I must have looked pretty _____appointed because Uncle Paul tried to cheer me up. He said, "I don't mean to be _____kind, but think about it. You wanted to read about unsolved mysteries, and I think you _____covered a real clue about the phantom and the missing pages!"

Scrambled Words. Unscramble the mixed-up words to make sense.

EXAMPLE:

1. There are <u>neesv</u> days in the week. _____*seven*_____
2. <u>tSras</u> twinkled in the sky. _____
3. <u>Rvreo</u> is a good name for a dog. _____
4. I have a <u>scta</u> on my broken arm. _____
5. I like <u>beard</u>, butter, and jam. _____
6. Horses live in <u>tabsles</u> on ranches. _____
7. School is out for the <u>urmsme</u>. _____
8. My foot hurts because my <u>hoes</u> is tight. _____
9. The duck quacked at the <u>rmaefr</u>. _____
10. Whales swim in the deep <u>eoacn</u>. _____
11. My <u>gradntmhoer</u> loves me very much. _____
12. I'm scared of <u>ssotnmre</u>. _____

Place Value. Write the numbers.

EX. 6 tens 8 ones **68**	1. 9 ones 4 tens _____	2. 5 tens 0 ones _____	3. 10 tens 0 ones _____
4. 6 tens 3 hundreds 8 ones _____	5. 4 hundreds 0 tens 2 ones _____	6. 5 ones 6 hundreds 7 tens _____	7. 9 hundreds 3 ones 5 tens _____

Write these numbers.

8. five hundred sixty-one _____

9. four hundred eighty-six _____

10. two hundred ninety-nine _____

11. eight hundred _____

12. one hundred fifty _____

13. seven hundred thirty-two _____

How many gumballs in each set?

Ex. 100 100 10 10 1   **221**

14. 100 100 100 100 10 1 _____

15. 100 100 10 1 1 1 _____

16. 100 100 100 10 10 10 _____

17. 100 10 10 10 1 1 _____

Divide these compound words into three categories. Write in cursive.

skyline
grapevine
raindrop
hindsight
drumstick
handbag
bluebell
landscape
oatmeal
suitcase
wishbone
hitchhike
goldfinch
themselves
limestone
showboat
thumbtack

1. long vowel combinations

_____
_____
_____
_____

2. short vowel combinations

_____
_____
_____
_____

3. long and short vowel combinations

_____
_____
_____
_____

Word Meanings. Write a word for each meaning.

| knead | sense | praise | dull | guide | amazing |
| wheat | coast | numb | certain | towel | purchase |

1. not able to feel   _____

2. we do this to dough   _____

3. to be sure   _____

4. to buy something   _____

5. to see, hear, feel, taste, smell   _____

6. flour is made from   _____

7. a leader of a group   _____

8. to say something nice   _____

9. something wonderful can be   _____

10. a knife that is not sharp   _____

11. where the ocean and the land meet _____

12. used to dry yourself   _____

Write the sentences that are true.

1. We are camping in the forest.
2. The wind is blowing the clouds at night.
3. It is raining.
4. We are fishing.
5. We are safe inside.

_____

_____

_____

_____

_____

How many ways can you make the amount of money shown in these problems? Use real money to help you.

Ex. <u>10¢</u>
10 pennies
2 nickels
1 nickel, 5 pennies
1 dime

1.   <u>25¢</u>

2.   <u>50¢</u>

3.   <u>$1.00</u>

4.   <u>$1.60</u>

5.   <u>$2.40</u>

Circle the nouns. Underline the verbs. Remember: Nouns name things and verbs show action.

elephant	sang	ate	fixed	laugh
beg	tent	Mr. Chip	team	
book	California	guitar	landed	Lake Street
freight	cleaned	yell	plays	
fly	visited	Kent	write	run
strength	swim	engine	jump	
broccoli	leap	letters	June	shakes
Marsha	dentist	friend	walk	

13

Use the word bank to make compound words answering the descriptions.

EXAMPLE:

Word Bank

~~bath~~	apple
space	storm
team	ship
horse	~~tub~~
snow	back
scare	side
post	card
hill	brows
eye	mates
pine	crow

1. A place your mom sends you to get clean. _bathtub_

2. A fruit that is good to eat._____

3. What farmers put in cornfields to scare birds away._____

4. A kind of weather some people get in the wintertime._____

5. If you ride on a horse, you have this kind of ride. _____

6. A place that might be grassy, high up, and a good place for a picnic._____

7. A type of mail you can write and send to a friend._____

8. People who play sports with you._____

9. What you should find on your face above your eyelashes._____

10. What astronauts might fly in._____

You are lost in the forest for a long time with nothing but a knife, a few matches, and one pan. How and where will you live? What will you do? What will you eat?

_____

_____

_____

_____

_____

_____

_____

_____

_____

_____

_____

Rounding Numbers. Round to the nearest ten.

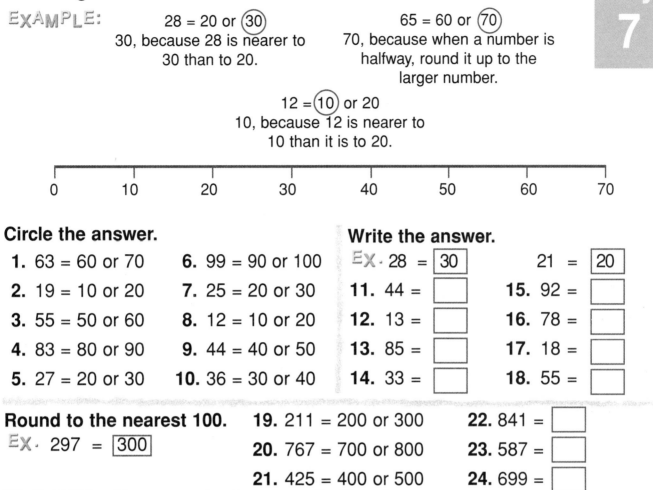

EXAMPLE:

28 = 20 or (30)
30, because 28 is nearer to
30 than to 20.

65 = 60 or (70)
70, because when a number is
halfway, round it up to the
larger number.

12 = (10) or 20
10, because 12 is nearer to
10 than it is to 20.

Number line: 0 10 20 30 40 50 60 70

Circle the answer.

1. 63 = 60 or 70
2. 19 = 10 or 20
3. 55 = 50 or 60
4. 83 = 80 or 90
5. 27 = 20 or 30

6. 99 = 90 or 100
7. 25 = 20 or 30
8. 12 = 10 or 20
9. 44 = 40 or 50
10. 36 = 30 or 40

Write the answer.

EX. 28 = [30]

11. 44 =
12. 13 =
13. 85 =
14. 33 =

21 = [20]

15. 92 =
16. 78 =
17. 18 =
18. 55 =

Round to the nearest 100.

EX. 297 = [300]

19. 211 = 200 or 300
20. 767 = 700 or 800
21. 425 = 400 or 500

22. 841 =
23. 587 =
24. 699 =

Rewrite this paragraph. Add the correct punctuation and capitalization.

last summer we went camping in colorado we went hiking and swimming every day one time i actually saw a little deer with spots and a white tail we also collected a lot of pretty rocks flowers and leaves we had a great time i didn't want to leave

_____

_____

_____

_____

_____

_____

_____

Circle the word that is divided into syllables correctly.

EXAMPLE: fi/fteen   (fif/teen)   fift/een   fifte/en

1. cact/us	ca/ctus	cac/tus	c/actus
2. bli/ster	blist/er	blis/ter	bl/ister
3. al/ways	a/lways	alw/ays	alwa/ys
4. har/bor	ha/rbor	harb/or	harbo/r
5. fl/ower	flo/wer	flowe/r	flow/er
6. bas/ket	bask/et	ba/sket	baske/t
7. e/nclose	en/close	encl/ose	enclo/se
8. obe/ys	o/beys	ob/eys	obey/s
9. qu/estion	quest/ion	que/stion	ques/tion
10. sal/ute	salut/e	sa/lute	salu/te

Write the abbreviation for the following words. Be sure to put a period (.) at the end of each abbreviation.

EXAMPLE:

1. January _____*Jan.*_____   10. Monday _____

2. February _____   11. Tuesday _____

3. March _____   12. Wednesday _____

4. April _____   13. Thursday _____

5. August _____   14. Saturday _____

6. October _____   15. Doctor _____

7. November _____   16. Mister _____

8. December _____   17. Mississippi _____

9. Sunday _____   18. Television _____

Be sure to look at the ones, tens, hundreds, and thousands as you do the following problems.

Which number is greater? Circle your answer.

1. 126	2. 342	3. 619
261	231	719

4. 1,426	5. 2,510	6. 1,629
1,326	3,510	1,639

Circle the number that is less.

7. 580	8. 999	9. 624
579	899	524

10. 1,200	11. 7,824	12. 5,555
1,201	7,842	5,846

Write greater than (>) or less than (<) on the line. EX. 521 __>__ than 121.

13. 267 is _____ than 367

14. 126 is _____ than 226

15. 808 is _____ than 801

16. 429 is _____ than 249

17. 762 is _____ than 761

18. 1,638 is _____ than 738

19. 4,206 is _____ than 5,206

20. 3,929 is _____ than 3,729

21. 5,340 is _____ than 5,940

22. 1,500 is _____ than 1,005

Read the following words.
Write the vowel you hear and mark if it's long or short.

EXAMPLE:	fly	ī	**long**
	went	ĕ	**short**

1. tie __ _____

2. puzzle __ _____

3. head __ _____

4. niece __ _____

5. bugle __ _____

6. plan __ _____

7. trail __ _____

8. chief __ _____

9. mule __ _____

10. toad __ _____

11. neck __ _____

12. high __ _____

13. sweat __ _____

14. bump __ _____

15. knot __ _____

16. ripped __ _____

17. find __ _____

18. chip __ _____

19. colt __ _____

20. sweep __ _____

21. patch __ _____

22. feather __ _____

23. juice __ _____

24. gray __ _____

Use commas, add small words, or leave words out to combine the sentences.

EXAMPLE:

1. My friends' names are Wanda and Pete. I also like Mandy and Joe.

I like my friends Wanda, Pete, Mandy, and Joe.

2. Rats will chew on wood and bones. They also will chew on nuts and twigs.

_____

3. Dogs and cats can be pets. Gerbils and hamsters can be pets, too.

_____

4. I am wearing blue jeans and a striped shirt. My shoes are black, and my socks are green. On my head is a baseball cap.

_____

_____

5. My teammates like ice cream, pie, and cake. They also like pizza, hamburgers, and hot dogs.

_____

_____

Read and follow directions. <u>Read them through completely first</u>. If you follow the directions carefully, you will find the name of an animal.

P L A E N H T E

1. Remove the letters L and the second E.
2. Put the LE at the beginning of the word.
3. Move the second E so it is at the beginning of the word.
4. Put an S at the end of the word.
5. Move the H so that it is between the P and the A.
6. Don't do step 4.
7. Write the name of the animal here.

_____

More Than Thousands.

We read:

> 6,000 — six thousand
> 60,000 — sixty thousand
> 600,000 — six hundred thousand

Read the following numbers aloud to a parent or an adult.

EXAMPLE:

50,231—fifty thousand two hundred thirty-one
765,326—seven hundred sixty-five thousand three hundred twenty-six

1. 92,126	**6.** 700,820	**11.** 7,069	**16.** 138,000
2. 9,800	**7.** 328,984	**12.** 942,681	**17.** 16,126
3. 87,124	**8.** 6,401	**13.** 31,010	**18.** 800,290
4. 3,823	**9.** 10,822	**14.** 575,618	**19.** 1,999
5. 40,000	**10.** 126,238	**15.** 202,435	**20.** 999,999

Make real words by writing ar, ir, or, er, ur, in the blanks.

h___se	n___se	th___ty	p___ch
h___d	ch___p	s___ve	b___ch
g___l	th___st	t___key	h___
ch___ge	c___b	m___ch	y___n
st___m	b___p	sp___k	sk___t
c___cus	c___n	rep___t	st___ch
th___sty	wh___l	al___m	t___n
p___se	g___m	c___l	f___st
b___st	f___m	v___b	ch___ch

ar

ir

or

er

ur

Build a super sandwich with the clues given and the ingredients listed.

Ingredients

pickles	ham	bologna	wheat bread
lettuce	beef	butter	sourdough bread
tomatoes	chicken	mustard	white bread
bean sprouts	pork	mayonnaise	rye bread

Clues

1. Make the sandwich using one kind of bread, two vegetables, and two meats.
2. Two ingredients should start with <u>b</u> and two with <u>p</u>.
3. Use the spread with the most letters in it.
4. Don't use anything that starts with <u>wh</u> or anything that ends in <u>f</u>.
5. Add a mystery ingredient to your sandwich. List the ingredients of your sandwich:

_____

_____

Draw and color your sandwich.

Put commas where they belong in the sentences.

EXAMPLE: August 10, 1970, and May 10, 1973, are birth dates in our family.

1. My parents were married in Portland Oregon on May 1 1959.
2. We had chicken potatoes corn gravy and ice cream for dinner.
3. George Washington became the first president on April 30 1789.
4. Sam was born June 16 1947 in Rome Italy.
5. We saw deer bear elk and goats on our trip.
6. On July 24 1962 in Boise Idaho I won the big race.
7. My best friends are Tom Mary Aaron Nan and Debra.
8. At the zoo we saw snakes elephants and bears.

Write your own series of words in these sentences. Put in the commas.

1. My favorite desserts are _____.
2. I wear _____ in the summer.
3. Some of my relatives are _____.

Column Addition.

				0	9	4	9
6	9	7	8	0	1	3	2
4	8	2	4	6	9	4	7
+2	+3	+8	+2	+3	+2	+2	+5

6 + 1 + 2 = _____   2 + 6 + 1 = _____   1 + 0 + 8 + 0 = _____

7 + 3 + 5 = _____   8 + 9 + 8 = _____   7 + 2 + 5 + 3 = _____

3 + 4 + 8 = _____   3 + 1 + 4 = _____   6 + 3 + 2 + 1 = _____

				32	15	73
18	41	32	25	41	30	12
20	20	11	24	12	12	62
+ 11	+ 16	+ 12	+ 20	+ 11	+ 42	+ 22

Verbs can tell what is happening now, or in the past. Write a correct verb in the blanks. If there is an **n** by the blank, write a "now" verb. If there is a **p** by the blank, write a "past" verb.

1. Two dogs (p) _____ each other down the road.

2. The wind (n) _____ and the trees (n) _____ .

3. We can (n) _____ and (n)_____ in the race.

4. Last night I (p) _____ past your house.

5. The hens (p) _____ at their food.

6. (n) _____ the kite string, please.

7. I (p) _____ at the jokes on TV last night.

8. Yesterday, we (p) _____ tulips and roses.

9. Mother (p) _____ all our dirty clothes.

10. I will (n) _____this job later.

Fill in the blanks with words that begin with bl-, fl-, br-, cl-, sn-, gl-, st-, cr-, sk-, gr-, sp-.

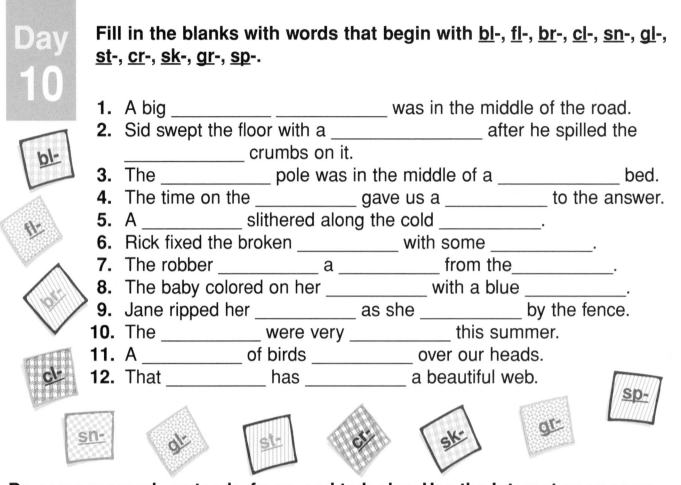

1. A big _____ _____ was in the middle of the road.
2. Sid swept the floor with a _____ after he spilled the _____ crumbs on it.
3. The _____ pole was in the middle of a _____ bed.
4. The time on the _____ gave us a _____ to the answer.
5. A _____ slithered along the cold _____.
6. Rick fixed the broken _____ with some _____.
7. The robber _____ a _____ from the_____.
8. The baby colored on her _____ with a blue _____.
9. Jane ripped her _____ as she _____ by the fence.
10. The _____ were very _____ this summer.
11. A _____ of birds _____ over our heads.
12. That _____ has _____ a beautiful web.

bl- fl- br- cl- sn- gl- st- cr- sk- gr- sp-

Do some research on toads, frogs, and tadpoles. Use the Internet or an encyclopedia. Then, draw six pictures to show, in order, how tadpoles change into frogs or toads.

1.

2.

3.

4.

5.

6.

Write the numbers that come after, before, or between.

1. 58, _____, 60

2. 80, _____, 82

3. _____, 19, 20

4. _____, 17, 18

5. _____, 10, _____

6. 151, _____, 153

7. 243, 244, _____

8. _____, 329, _____

9. 429, _____, _____

10. 869, _____, 871

11. 619, _____, _____

12. _____, 888, _____

13. _____, 500, _____

14. 209, _____, _____

15. 721, _____, 723

16. _____, _____, 307

17. _____, 398, _____

18. 900, _____, _____

19. _____, 200, _____

20. 998, 999, _____

21. _____,1,201

22. 2,429, _____

23. 6,000, _____

24. _____, 9,930

25. _____, 4,000

26. 7,822, _____

27. 5,001, _____

28. _____, 3,030

29. _____, 7,842

30. 9,999, _____

Number these phrases in order so they make sense.

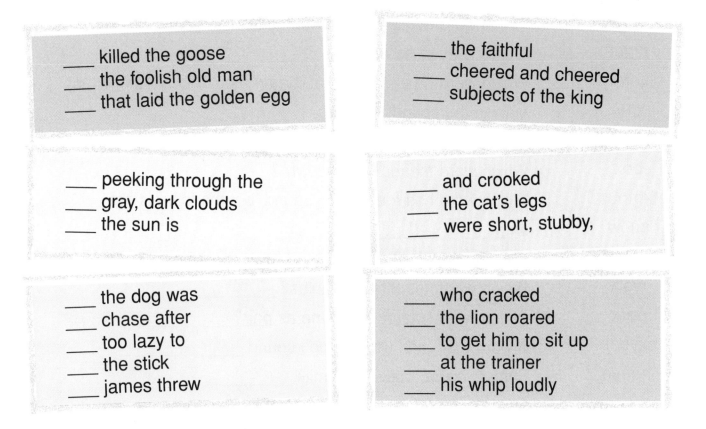

_____ killed the goose
_____ the foolish old man
_____ that laid the golden egg

_____ the faithful
_____ cheered and cheered
_____ subjects of the king

_____ peeking through the
_____ gray, dark clouds
_____ the sun is

_____ and crooked
_____ the cat's legs
_____ were short, stubby,

_____ the dog was
_____ chase after
_____ too lazy to
_____ the stick
_____ james threw

_____ who cracked
_____ the lion roared
_____ to get him to sit up
_____ at the trainer
_____ his whip loudly

Read the paragraph, and circle the answers to the questions.

Many enormous bones have been found. Scientists have put them together to make dinosaur skeletons. Fossils of other extinct animals and plants have also been found. You can see dinosaur skeletons and other fossils in many museums.

1. The main idea of the paragraph is
   a. museums.
   b. fossils.

2. The word <u>them</u> in the paragraph stands for
   a. skeletons.
   b. dinosaurs.
   c. bones.

3. The word <u>enormous</u> means
   a. huge.
   b. hungry.
   c. little.

4. In this paragraph, <u>extinct</u> means
   a. happy to be alive.
   b. not alive anymore.
   c. very big animals.

5. Would you like to be a scientist?   yes   no

Study these words and fill in the blanks with the correct words.

night
different
dry
knock
box
famous
snow
hopped
walk
pear
oxygen
cheese

1. Which word begins with a silent letter?_____

2. This is a weather word._____

3. Which word has a <u>t</u> sound at the end, but it is not the letter <u>t</u> making the sound?_____

4. Which word has a silent <u>gh</u>?_____

5. Which word means "well-known"?_____

6. Which word has the short <u>o</u> sound, but the letter is not an <u>o</u>?_____

7. What do we breathe?_____

8. Which word has three syllables?_____

9. Which word sounds the same as <u>pair</u>?_____

10. A word that ends with a long <u>i</u> sound._____

11. Something we make from milk._____

12. A word we add -<u>es</u> to so it means more than one._____

See if you can figure out these story problems.

1. Ten children are in line to get a drink. Debra is ninth. How many children are in front of her?

_____

2. How many days are between the 18th and the 28th day of the month?

_____

3. There are 20 horses in a race. Prince is next to last. Name his place in the race.

_____

4. If Ted is next to last in line, and he is also tenth from the first person in line, how many children are in line?

_____

5. What are the "teen" numbers?

_____, _____, _____,

_____, _____, _____,

_____

6. How old will you be 15 years from now?

_____

7. Twenty-five children are in line. Only one is a girl. She is in the middle of the line. How many boys are in front of her and how many behind her?

_____

8. If today was the 22nd of June, what date will it be one week from today?

_____

9. Jack is 16th in line. How many people are ahead of him?

_____

The <u>subject</u> of a sentence tells <u>who</u> or <u>what</u> the sentence is about. The <u>predicate</u> of a sentence tells something about the subject. Both can have more than one word, or just one word.

Circle the (subject) of the following sentences, and underline the <u>predicate</u>.

EXAMPLE:

1. (Our team) <u>won the game</u>.
2. Clowns make me laugh.
3. We started to swim.
4. Chris worked in his garden.
5. Bees can sting people.
6. Mom and I rode our horses.
7. Chickens lay eggs daily.
8. Ducks eat lots of worms.
9. Children are sometimes mean.
10. She has a hoop.
11. A little red fox ran by us.
12. April lost her house keys.
13. Lions live in cages.
14. I found twenty-five cents.
15. This ruler is one foot long.
16. We went on a picnic.
17. Birds make nests for their eggs.
18. The king rode a bike.
19. My friends walk every day.
20. Sammy is always hungry.

Day 12

Write the word that does not belong with the other words in the row. Then describe why the other words belong together. The first one is done for you.

EXAMPLE:

1. rose, daisy, lazy, tulip, lily   *lazy*   *the others are flowers*
2. newspaper, book, television, magazine   _____ _____
3. hand, eye, foot, hose   _____ _____
4. tuba, clarinet, jazz, flute, harp   _____ _____
5. poets, farmers, authors, whales, teachers   _____ _____
6. tire, hammer, screwdriver, wrench   _____ _____
7. robin, hawk, sparrow, pig, jay   _____ _____
8. John, Tom, Robert, Jenny, Todd   _____ _____
9. Moon, Mars, Earth, Pluto, Venus   _____ _____
10. lettuce, peach, carrot, peas, beets   _____ _____
11. Mary, Jane, Susan, Ann, George   _____ _____
12. May, Tuesday, January, June, July   _____ _____

Use the apostrophe correctly. Change each underlined word or phrase by using the apostrophe.

EXAMPLE:

1. <u>You</u> <u>are</u> a good piano player.   *You're*
2. This is my <u>grandmothers</u> pet dog.   _____
3. The <u>monsters</u> eyes are green.   _____
4. The boy <u>will</u> <u>not</u> make his bed.   _____
5. The girl <u>would</u> <u>not</u> help her friend.   _____
6. I borrowed <u>Nancys</u> swimming suit.   _____
7. Boyd does not have a <u>catchers</u> mitt.   _____
8. <u>It</u> <u>is</u> so hot during the summer.   _____
9. The <u>newspapers</u> reporter writes about the news.   _____
10. <u>Kellys</u> dog has fleas.   _____

Adding 2-Digit Numbers. Remember to trade or regroup in the ones column.

EXAMPLE:

1							
26	62	18	45	73	42	19	12
+ 37	+ 19	+ 27	+ 38	+ 19	+ 29	+ 9	+ 3
63							

56	66	14	37	16	38	29	59
+ 57	+ 55	+ 26	+ 33	+ 85	+ 32	+ 55	+ 7

96¢	46¢	98¢	95¢	56¢	17¢	11¢	18¢
+ 56¢	+ 64¢	+ 84¢	+ 85¢	+ 26¢	+ 17¢	+ 99¢	+ 18¢

Read the sentences carefully. Look at the underlined word in each sentence. Choose another word or words that mean the same as the underlined word.

EXAMPLE:

1. Will you <u>repay</u> the money I lent you? _____return_____

2. The oak tree is <u>afire</u>. _____

3. Sara fell down outside, but she was <u>unhurt</u>. _____

4. I would like to <u>revisit</u> Disneyland sometime. _____

5. I think this birthday list is <u>incomplete</u>. _____

6. This lovely painted picture is <u>unfinished</u>. _____

7. Do not <u>uncover</u> the dough or it will dry out. _____

8. Don't use this phone; it's only for <u>incoming</u> calls. _____

9. This paper is really <u>important</u>. _____

10. This part of the forest remains <u>untouched</u>. _____

11. Every few years we <u>repaint</u> the school. _____

12. I <u>dislike</u> cake and ice cream. _____

Add a suffix to the following words. Use -est, -tion, -ty. At the end, write three sentences. Choose three different words with three different suffixes. Remember to double, drop, or change some letters.

1. taste _tastiest_
2. safe _____
3. prepare _____
4. sad _____
5. dirt _____
6. tall _____

7. act _____
8. hungry _____
9. heavy _____
10. direct _____
11. invent _____
12. nine _____

1. _____
2. _____
3. _____

Is and are tell that something is happening now. Use is with singular subjects, are with plural subjects.

1. Max and I _____ best friends.
2. Bill _____ also our friend.
3. We _____ all going camping this summer.
4. Meg _____ coming with us.
5. Her sister _____ coming, too.
6. My pet _____ a big, black snake.
7. Those bananas _____ very ripe.
8. How old _____ the children?

are

is

Write your own sentences now. Write two using is, two using are.

1. is _____
2. are _____
3. is _____
4. are _____

Arrange the numbers from <u>greatest</u> to <u>least</u>.

1. 261   325   496   547   _____ _____ _____ _____
2. 746   793   733   779   _____ _____ _____ _____
3. 596   579   588   499   _____ _____ _____ _____
4. 496   649   964   946   _____ _____ _____ _____
5. 846   808   903   778   _____ _____ _____ _____

Arrange the numbers from <u>least</u> to <u>greatest</u>.

1. 764   674   746   647   _____ _____ _____ _____
2. 503   530   353   550   _____ _____ _____ _____
3. 940   490   904   409   _____ _____ _____ _____
4. 883   838   388   880   _____ _____ _____ _____
5. 676   767   690   719   _____ _____ _____ _____

Write these words in alphabetical order. Be sure to look at the first, second, and third letters. Write them in cursive.

wash	school	eye	do	does
large	brought	spread	often	you
enough	front	people	breakfast	neighbor

1. _____   6. _____   11. _____
2. _____   7. _____   12. _____
3. _____   8. _____   13. _____
4. _____   9. _____   14. _____
5. _____   10. _____   15. _____

Sequence.

Denise and Grayson washed their dad's car. First, they filled a bucket with soapy water. Denise got some old rags from the house while Grayson got the hose. They put soapy water all over the car and washed off the dirt. Next, they sprayed the car with water. To finish the job, Denise and Grayson wiped the car dry with some clean towels. Both of them were surprised when their dad gave them each $5.

Write four sentences about the story in the correct order.

1. _____

2. _____

3. _____

4. _____

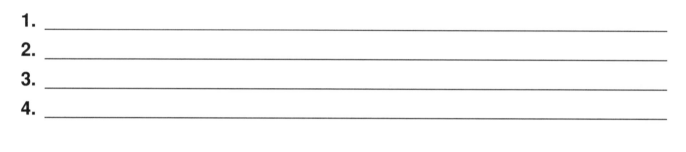

-est, -tion, and -ty are suffixes. The word list below contains words using suffixes. Read them and write the base word on the line.

EXAMPLE:

1. safety _____*safe*_____

2. hungriest _____

3. invention _____

4. location _____

5. loveliest _____

6. preparation _____

7. reality _____

8. hottest _____

9. starvation _____

10. action _____

11. certainty _____

12. direction _____

13. saddest _____

14. tasty _____

15. suggestion _____

16. wettest _____

Equal Groups.

EXAMPLE:

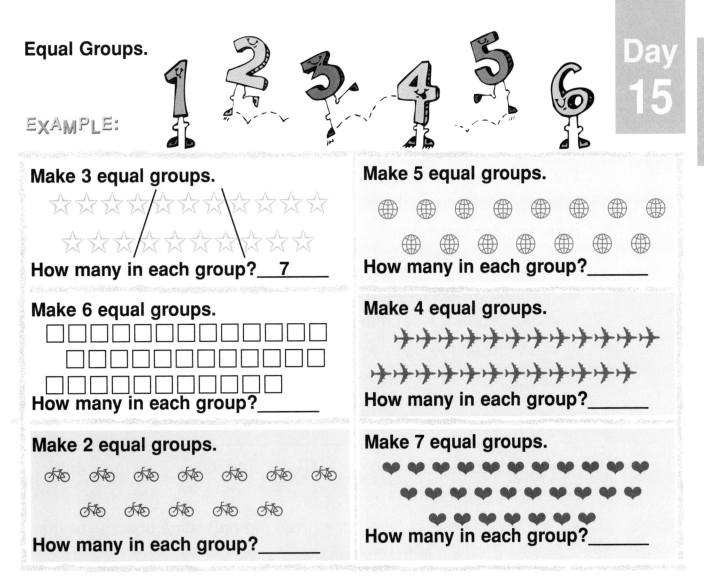

Make 3 equal groups.

How many in each group?___7___

Make 5 equal groups.

How many in each group?_____

Make 6 equal groups.

How many in each group?_____

Make 4 equal groups.

How many in each group?_____

Make 2 equal groups.

How many in each group?_____

Make 7 equal groups.

How many in each group?_____

Use <u>who's</u>, <u>whose</u> in the first four blanks and <u>you're</u>, <u>your</u> in the next four.

"_____ making all the racket?" shouted the king.

"_____ footprints are those in the garden?"

"_____ going to solve this mystery for the king?"

"_____ turn is it to help the king?"

"What is _____ favorite food?" asked the dinner guest.

"Rabbit stew!" answered the host. "_____ going to eat it tonight for dinner."

"Great!" gulped the rabbit. "_____ going to have to give me _____ recipe."

Who do you think is in the king's garden? _____

_____

How do you think the rabbit really felt about rabbit stew?

_____

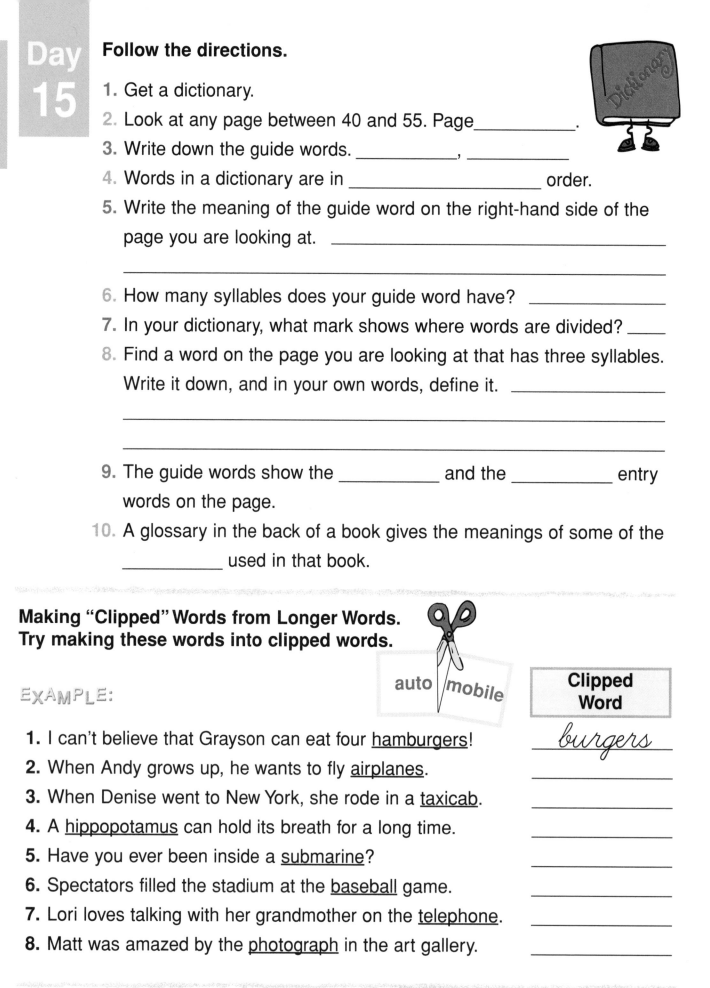

Day 15

Follow the directions.

1. Get a dictionary.
2. Look at any page between 40 and 55. Page_____.
3. Write down the guide words. _____, _____
4. Words in a dictionary are in _____ order.
5. Write the meaning of the guide word on the right-hand side of the page you are looking at. _____

   _____

6. How many syllables does your guide word have? _____
7. In your dictionary, what mark shows where words are divided? ____
8. Find a word on the page you are looking at that has three syllables. Write it down, and in your own words, define it. _____

   _____

   _____

9. The guide words show the _____ and the _____ entry words on the page.
10. A glossary in the back of a book gives the meanings of some of the _____ used in that book.

Making "Clipped" Words from Longer Words.
Try making these words into clipped words.

EXAMPLE: auto | mobile

	Clipped Word
	burgers

1. I can't believe that Grayson can eat four <u>hamburgers</u>!
2. When Andy grows up, he wants to fly <u>airplanes</u>.
3. When Denise went to New York, she rode in a <u>taxicab</u>.
4. A <u>hippopotamus</u> can hold its breath for a long time.
5. Have you ever been inside a <u>submarine</u>?
6. Spectators filled the stadium at the <u>baseball</u> game.
7. Lori loves talking with her grandmother on the <u>telephone</u>.
8. Matt was amazed by the <u>photograph</u> in the art gallery.

Words to Sound, Read, and Spell

able	cousin	grown	nothing	stretch
above	cover	guess	number	strong
address	daily	guest	ocean	sudden
afraid	daughter	half	often	sugar
again	dead	happen	once	sure
ahead	dear	heard	only	surprise
alley	decide	height	oven	sword
along	dictionary	here	parade	taken
already	does	hour	paste	taught
always	done	huge	pear	tear
another	dozen	hundred	people	tenth
answer	drawer	hungry	please	their
around	early	instead	poem	thousand
aunt	earn	iron	prayer	thread
awake	engine	island	present	threw
awful	enough	juice	probably	through
bathe	every	knee	promise	tied
beautiful	except	know	proud	tired
because	famous	ladder	quiet	together
become	fare	language	receive	tomorrow
begin	favorite	large	remember	trouble
behind	feather	library	rhyme	truly
believe	fence	lightning	safety	tunnel
bottle	finish	listen	said	twenty
bought	fire	lose	sandwich	until
breakfast	forget	matter	says	use
breath	forty	maybe	school	usual
brother	fourth	meant	scratch	visit
brought	fresh	middle	sense	wagon
build	friend	minute	seventy	welcome
busy	frighten	money	sew	were
buy	front	month	share	where
caught	fruit	morning	silence	wire
cheese	garage	nature	similar	without
chief	garden	neighbor	sincerely	woman
children	giant	nickel	sixth	women
close	glove	niece	smooth	your
cloth	goes	nineteen	soldiers	
color	gone	ninety	some	
cough	grammar	ninth	sorry	
course	growl	none	special	

Words to Sound, Read, and Spell

accident	announcement	bandleader	blew	build
ached	annoyed	banner	blinded	builder
aching	another	barbed	blizzard	building
acorns	answered	barely	blocked	bulb
acrobatic	anxiously	barnyard	blond	bulldozer
across	anybody	baseball	blood	bunch
action	anymore	basic	blueberry	bunk
active	anyone	basket	board	burdensome
actually	anything	bathroom	bobbing	buried
admire	anyway	bathtub	body	burned
admitted	anywhere	batteries	bold	business
advice	apartment	beach	bolted	bustle
afraid	apologize	beanpole	bones	busy
afternoon	applause	beasts	bookcase	butcher
against	applesauce	beautiful	bored	butterfly
agent	apply	became	born	cabin
ages	approaches	because	borrows	cable
agree	area	bedroom	bossy	cactus
agreement	aren't	beehive	bother	cage
ahead	argument	beetles	bottle	calm
airline	around	before	bottom	came
airport	arrangements	began	bought	camera
alarmed	arrive	begged	bounce	candlemaker
alike	arriving	begin	bounded	candles
alive	arrow	beginning	bracelets	cannon
alligator	artist	behind	branches	cannot
allowed	ashamed	believe	brave	can't
almond	aside	belong	bravely	cape
almost	asked	below	bread	captain
alone	asleep	beneath	break	cardboard
along	attention	bench	breakfast	cardinal
aloud	audience	beside	breath	cared
alphabet	author	besides	breed	carefully
already	awake	between	breeze	carpenter
although	awful	bigger	brilliant	carried
always	awoke	biggest	bristling	carrier
amazement	babbled	birthday	broke	carrot
amazing	backwards	blackberries	brood	carry
among	backyard	blackberry	brook	cartoon
ancient	badly	blackness	brother	carved
anger	baking	blanketed	brought	castle
angrily	balconies	blankets	brush	catch
animal	balloons	blast	bubbles	
ankles	bandage	blaze	bucket	
announced	bandages	bleeding	buggy	

Summer Bridge Activities™

Incentive Contract Calendar

Month _____

My parents and I decided that if I complete 20 days of
Summer Bridge Activities™ and read _____ minutes a day,
my incentive/reward will be:

_____

Child's Signature _____
Parent's Signature _____

Day 1	📖	⭐	___
Day 2	📖	⭐	___
Day 3	📖	⭐	___
Day 4	📖	⭐	___
Day 5	📖	⭐	___
Day 6	📖	⭐	___
Day 7	📖	⭐	___
Day 8	📖	⭐	___
Day 9	📖	⭐	___
Day 10	📖	⭐	___
Day 11	📖	⭐	___
Day 12	📖	⭐	___
Day 13	📖	⭐	___
Day 14	📖	⭐	___
Day 15	📖	⭐	___
Day 16	📖	⭐	___
Day 17	📖	⭐	___
Day 18	📖	⭐	___
Day 19	📖	⭐	___
Day 20	📖	⭐	___

Child: Color the ⭐ for daily activities completed.
Color the 📖 for daily reading completed.

Parent: Initial the _____ for daily activities and reading
your child completes.

Fun Activity Ideas to Go Along with the Second Section!

1. Find a pen pal; send him/her a letter.

2. Check if garden peas are ripe.

3. Great day for a family or neighborhood water fight.

4. Select a topic of interest—go to the library and check out three books on the topic.

5. Build a small wooden boat and use during a gutter-gushing thunderstorm.

6. Plan a bike hike with your family.

7. Visit a local children's museum.

8. Collect twenty assorted bugs and identify them.

9. Weed a row in the garden. (Mom and Dad will love you for it!)

10. Eat some French fries—learn a French phrase: *s'il vous plaît*.

11. Play "capture the flag" under a full moon.

12. Visit a ghost town.

13. Research some trivia—collect some information at the library and surprise your family.

14. Do something ecological—clean up an area near your house. Make your planet better.

15. Get a "knothole" pass to a local baseball or softball game.

16. Arrange photo albums.

17. Make fruit juice bars and freeze them.

18. Learn sign language or Morse code.

19. Go to a planetarium and see a star show.

20. Time to paint the fence. (Ever heard of Tom Sawyer?)

Find the differences. Be sure to trade or regroup.

EXAMPLE:

```
  7 10      6 12
  8̸0̸       7̸2̸        64      23      70      43      77      53
 - 29       - 7       - 57     - 9     - 23    - 14    - 28    - 33
  51        65
```

```
  63      91      38      81      55      82      25      40
 - 45     - 42    - 19    - 15     - 9    - 16    - 16    - 21
```

```
  68      76      75      85      50      31      44      91
 - 39     - 37     - 7    - 17    - 24    - 15    - 36    - 73
```

Go to the library and get a book you have not read. After you finish reading it, write a book report. Use the outline below to help you.

1. Title _____

2. Author _____

3. Main characters _____

_____

4. Setting: Where does the story take place? _____

5. Main idea: What is the book about? _____

_____

_____

_____

_____

6. Did you like the book? _____ Why or why not? _____

_____

_____

Fill in the blanks. Use the words in the Word Box.

Word Box

nonsense	repeat	journey	debts
skillet	cottage	fortune	greedy
clever	cabbage	wisdom	judge
frame	original	collect	especially

1. My brother will _____ the money for us.
2. Mother put the _____ in a large _____ to cook.
3. This is an _____ painting.
4. I read a story about a very _____ giant.
5. Some people think it's _____ to be afraid of the dark.
6. The elf played a _____ trick on me.
7. Will you please _____ what you just said?
8. My uncle made his _____ by working in a coal mine.
9. Joe made this gift _____ for you.
10. The woodsman lived in a _____ next to the forest.
11. My aunt is going on a long _____ by train.
12. Did John make the _____ for the picture?
13. The _____ told the man he had to pay his _____.
14. A wise person has a lot of _____.

Quotation marks set off what a person or thing says.
Put quotation marks around what these people say.

EXAMPLE: **: Mom said, "Don't do that!"**

1. Uncle Bill said, I will pack a picnic lunch.
2. Where is the big beach ball? asked Jeff.
3. Lily exclaimed, That's a wonderful idea!
4. Complaining will not help you, replied Dad.
5. Come and do your work, Grandmother said, or you can't go with us.
6. Yesterday, said Emily, I saw a pretty robin in a tree by my window.
7. I will always take care of my pets, promised Ted.
8. Come and get this puppy off my newspaper! yelled Dad.
9. Rachel said, Maybe we should have practiced more.
10. Dr. Jake asked, How are you, Pat? My ears hurt, Pat answered sadly.
11. It's a beautiful afternoon, said Paul.
12. Jed explained, My family is having a party.

Using Grids.

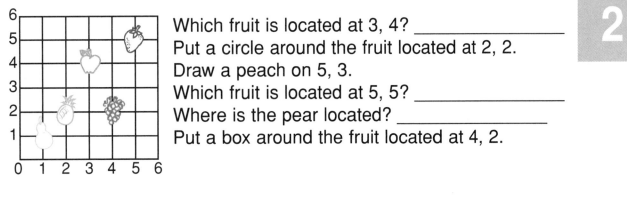

Which fruit is located at 3, 4? _____
Put a circle around the fruit located at 2, 2.
Draw a peach on 5, 3.
Which fruit is located at 5, 5? _____
Where is the pear located? _____
Put a box around the fruit located at 4, 2.

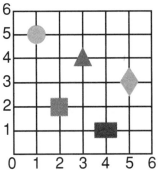

Which shape is located at 3, 4? _____
Where is the square located? _____
Draw a circle around the shape located at 3, 4.
Draw a line to connect the shapes located at 4, 1 and 1, 5.

Nouns. Common nouns are general names for places, things, and people. **Proper nouns** name a specific person, place, or thing and begin with a capital letter.

EXAMPLE:

Put these nouns under the right heading and then write four of your own. Be sure to use capital letters on the proper nouns.

Proper Nouns	Common Nouns
1. *Mrs. Jones*	1. *teacher*
2.	2.
3.	3.
4.	4.
5.	5.
6.	6.
7.	7.
8.	8.
9.	9.
10.	10.
11.	11.
12.	12.
13.	13.
14.	14.
15.	15.

salt lake   dog
monday   ocean
pet   oak street
day   class
november   holiday
mr. brown   christmas
boston   boat
beans   rex
apple   florida
school   dr. phil

Read this paragraph and then answer the questions.

Before you decide what kind of pet you would like to own, there are some things you need to think about. First, you need to find out how much care the pet would need. Dogs need to be walked; horses need to be exercised; cats need a place to scratch. All pets need to be kept clean and well fed. You need to think about where your pet would live. Big pets need a lot of room, while little pets don't need as much room.

1. What is the topic?
  a. caring for a dog
  b. choosing a pet
  c. feeding big pets

2. What is the main idea?
  a. finding a good home for pets
  b. things you need to do when choosing a pet
  c. things you need to think about before choosing a pet

3. What pet do you own or would you like to own?

_____

Read these silly sentences and then make your own silly sentences. Try to use the same starting letter for most of the words in each sentence.

1. Silly Sandra sells sweet sandwiches sprinkled with sugar.
2. Bill Benson built a boat with beetle-bitten birch bark.

_____
_____
_____
_____
_____
_____
_____
_____
_____
_____
_____

Add or subtract. Check the signs. Trade or regroup if you need to.

EXAMPLE:

1	512					
$8.54	$6.25	$7.42	$8.70	$3.69	$9.60	$7.38
+ 1.60	- 1.84	- 1.16	- 6.30	- 1.25	+ 1.92	+ 1.43
$10.14	$4.41					

575	600	804	133	202	623	101
- 162	+ 197	+ 129	- 124	- 102	+ 527	- 32

289	211	555	475	758	908	537
+ 428	+ 429	- 326	+ 482	- 523	+ 129	- 429

Discover the secret message by starting with the letters in the first vertical row. Record each letter in that row in order; then do the same thing with the remaining rows.

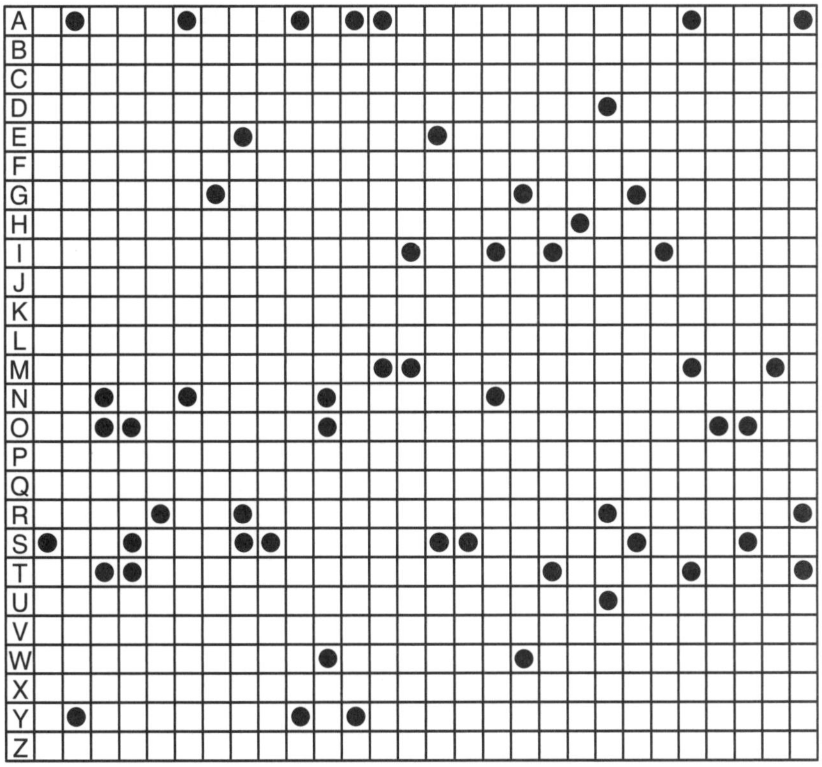

Secret messages for a Super Kid

— — — — — — —

— — — — — — — — — .

— — — — — — — —

— — —

— — — — — — —

— — — — — — — — — — .

— — — — — —

— — — — !

Sequencing. Read this story; then number the sentences in the order they happened.

Last summer, on our way to camp, the bus broke down. Our driver was able to get the bus off the road before it stopped. We were asked to stay on the bus and sit quietly in our seats. We stayed in our seats, but we were not quiet. We sang camp songs and camp chants that we learned at camp the year before.

A policeman came by and called for help on his radio. It took about an hour before another bus came to take us the rest of the way. It was a newer bus, and it wasn't long before we were choosing what bed we were going to sleep in, instead of what seat we were going to sit in on the bus.

- ☐ We sang songs and chants while waiting for another bus.
- ☐ Our bus broke down on our way to camp.
- ☐ Another bus came by to take us to camp.
- ☐ We chose what bed to sleep in.
- ☐ A policeman came by and radioed for help.

Here are some often misspelled words. Practice them; then spell them to a friend. Be sure to write in cursive. Write each word at least four times.

wonderful	_____
warm	_____
worried	_____
who	_____
where	_____
weigh	_____
want	_____
won't	_____
was	_____
word	_____
watch	_____
wash	_____

Ways of Writing the Same Concept. Circle the right answers to the problems.

1. How many balls in all?

a. 5 + 5 + 5
b. 3 + 5 + 5
c. 5 x 3
d. 3 + 3 + 3 + 3

2. How many stars in all?

a. 3 x 6
b. 6 + 6 + 6
c. 4 + 4 + 4 + 2
d. 6 x 3

3. How many boxes in all?

a. 5 + 8
b. 8 x 5
c. 8 + 8 + 8 + 8 + 8
d. 5 + 5 + 5 + 5 + 5

4. How many flowers in all?

a. 2 + 2 + 2 + 2 + 2 + 2 + 2 + 2 + 2
b. 9 x 2
c. 9 + 6
d. 2 x 9

Think of some verbs for the following sentences and write them in the blanks.

1. The kittens were _____ in circles.
2. The parakeets have _____ all their food.
3. Andrew is _____ the piano.
4. Dad _____ the car yesterday.
5. The puppy _____ under the porch.
6. I _____ the answer, but I was afraid to raise my hand.
7. Kelly will _____ the calves some oats.
8. Our club will _____ seeds to make some money.
9. My father has _____ to Texas.
10. The airplane was _____ at the airport.
11. Mother _____ the cake into ten pieces.
12. Travis _____ his bike twenty miles a week.
13. Books _____ us many things.
14. She _____ a lot of photographs while she was on her trip.

Choose the correct homonym to complete the sentence.

1. Jennifer has two _____ and three oranges. **pears   pairs**

2. Brian can never _____ to play the game right. **seam   seem**

3. Mother will sift the _____ for the cookies. **flour   flower**

4. For twelve _____, Angela has been trying to bake brownies.
   days   daze

5. I hope that I can get everything _____ on time. **write   right**

6. Nanette _____ the baking contest. **won   one**

7. Twice this year, the teacher _____ over her project.
   past   passed

8. The bread _____ was very sticky. **dough   doe**

9. I tasted a _____ of southern fried chicken. **piece   peace**

10. Did you ever _____ who won the contest? **hear   here**

11. Jana was _____ a dollar for a late book. **fined   find**

12. The painting of the picture was _____, but not excellent.
    fare   fair

You have designed a float for the Independence Day parade. Describe it in detail and tell who will ride on it.

_____

_____

_____

_____

_____

_____

_____

_____

_____

_____

_____

_____

Thinking about Time.

1. What time does the clock show?

   _____

2. How long does it take for the minute hand to move from 6 to 5? _____

3. What time will it be when the minute hand reaches the 12?

   _____

4. What time will it be when the minute hand moves 15 minutes?

   _____

Read the sentences and fill in the blanks with words that use two different sounds of <u>ow</u>.

<u>ow</u>

1. A scarecr_____ really works to keep birds away from the corn. A bird was here awhile ago, but he has fl_____n away.

2. You have been playing outside and are so dirty that you need a sh_____er. Here is a clean washcloth and t_____el to use.

3. I need to use a lawn m_____er to cut our grass. It has gr_____n so tall.

4. The king wears a gold cr_____n on his head, and his wife, the queen, wears a beautiful g_____n.

5. You have food on your face just above your eyebr_____. Don't fr_____n, just wash it off!

Read this story.

One day a lad was chopping wood in a forest. All at once, he heard a muffled sound coming from behind a tree. He stopped chopping, walked over to the tree, and peeked behind it. He could not believe his eyes. Right there, at the foot of the tree, an elf was hiding a pot of gold.

Circle a, b, or c to answer.

1. In this story, <u>muffled</u> means
   a. not to make a loud sound.
   b. to keep warm.
   c. to gag someone.

2. Another word for <u>forest</u>
   a. big logs.
   b. a few trees.
   c. woods.

3. <u>Lad</u> is another name for
   a. girl.
   b. boy.
   c. man.

4. A word in the story that sounds like <u>herd</u> is _____.

5. The word <u>he</u> stands for
   a. the elf.
   b. the tree.
   c. the lad.

How many words can you make out of <u>Independence</u> <u>Day</u>?

EXAMPLE:

depend
end

Multiplication. Finish the charts.

X2	
4	
8	
3	6
6	
9	
5	10
7	

X3	
3	9
7	
5	
2	
6	18
4	
8	

X4	
10	
5	20
8	
4	
7	
6	
9	

X5	
9	
2	
6	
3	15
5	
7	
4	

Use a word from the box to complete each sentence. Divide the word by what you know about syllables.

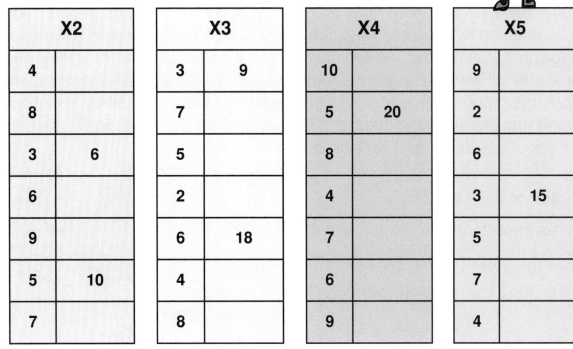

| trumpet |
| cottage |
| circus |
| giggle |
| butcher |
| pictures |
| market |
| quarter |
| signal |
| pennies |
| chatter |
| curtains |

EXAMPLE:

1. I am learning to play the __trum·pet__ .
2. Look at all the funny _____ in this book.
3. You can buy bread and milk at the _____.
4. We live in a small _____.
5. This pencil costs a _____.
6. I am saving lots of _____ in a jar.
7. The clowns at the _____ were great.
8. When you hear the _____, run fast.
9. We have white _____ on our window.
10. Chipmunks _____.
11. The _____ cuts meat to sell.
12. The girls started to _____.

Read the story and answer the questions at the end.

Reading a newspaper is a fun activity. It is also an important way to learn about what's going on in the world around you. Newspapers tell you who is doing what—and often, why they are doing it. There is a weather page to tell you what the weather is going to be like the next day and probably all week. The sports section usually tells you what games are coming up and what teams won yesterday. Newspapers tell us about our world leaders and what happens in their countries. Newspapers also tell us about accidents and serious events.

Why did the author write this?

a. to give us important facts about newspapers

b. to tell us that newspapers are make-believe

c. to tell us about the weather and sports

Practice writing and spelling -<u>ing</u> words. Write in cursive.

starting

hiking

stopping

breathing

sneezing

blooming

breaking

speaking

hearing

listening

spelling

working

running

walking

fighting

Make up and write some of your own -<u>ing</u> words.

EXAMPLE:

hitting

napping

Draw a line through three numbers that add up to the sum given in each diagram below.

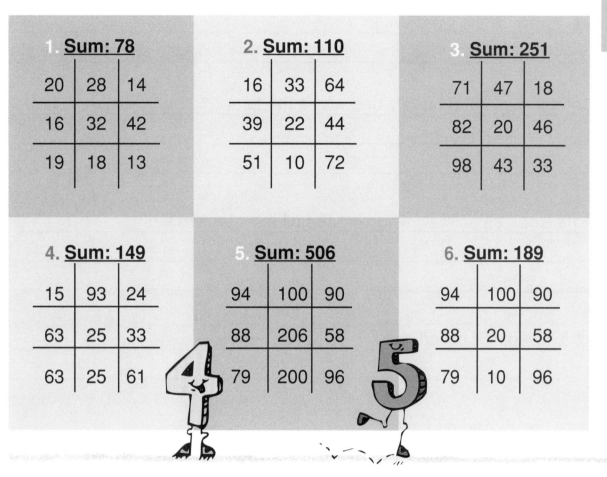

1. Sum: 78

20	28	14
16	32	42
19	18	13

2. Sum: 110

16	33	64
39	22	44
51	10	72

3. Sum: 251

71	47	18
82	20	46
98	43	33

4. Sum: 149

15	93	24
63	25	33
63	25	61

5. Sum: 506

94	100	90
88	206	58
79	200	96

6. Sum: 189

94	100	90
88	20	58
79	10	96

Use the correct form of the verb—past or present.

1. My friends and I like to _____ clay animals. (**make**)

2. We _____ the clay into different shapes. (**roll**)

3. Jeremy _____ making a clay hippo. (**enjoy**)

4. Our teacher _____ us fire the clay animals. (**help**)

5. He _____ them all in the kiln. (**place**)

6. After they were fired, we _____ them. (**paint**)

7. Often we _____ them as gifts. (**give**)

8. Marcus _____ his broken glass hippo because he thought he could fix it. (**keep**)

9. We all said we would _____ them again sometime. (**make**)

10. Marcus _____ he wouldn't break his the next time we did them. (**hope**)

These sentences are mixed up. Write them in cursive the correct way. Don't forget capitals and punctuation marks.

1. rolled hill the we down in a car

_____

_____

2. was car no but hurt wreck luckily one was a the total

_____

_____

3. themselves elephant animals when braced all the sneezed the

_____

_____

4. bottles of full wagon a pulled cory

_____

_____

5. book went I bed closed and my to

_____

_____

6. bob farm chicken uncle a has my

_____

See if you can read this story. You might want to cross out a certain letter.

FranniesFrogslivessinsyonderspond.sFranniesFrogswassasfriendlys frog.sSheslikesstossingswiththesothersfrogssthatslivesinsyonder spond.sOnesproblem,sthough,sissthatseverystimesFranniesFrogsstarts stossingswithsallsthesothersfrogs,sshessingsstoosloud.sFrannies Frogsisssuchsasnoisysfrogsthatsshesdrownssoutsallsthesotherscroaks. sNosothersfrogsissassloud.sFrannie'sscroakscansbesheardsforsmiles sandsmiles.sFranniesFrogsalsoslikesstossitsaroundsandseatsbugs. sThesothersfrogsscan'tscatchsbugssassfastsassFrannie,ssoswhens Frannieeatsswithsthesothersfrogs,ssheseatssthesmost!sThesothers frogssusuallyswaitsuntilsFranniesissfinishedsbeforestheyscansgetsfull.s Frannieshassaslotsofsfriends,sbutsFranniesFrogsissonesfunny,sfat, snoisy,sfriendlysfrog.

Continue the counting pattern.

```
1.    0     3     6     9    12   ___  ___  ___   24  ___
2.    6    12    18    24   ___  ___  ___   48  ___  ___
3.   12    16    20    24   ___  ___  ___   44  ___
4.   33    30    27    24   ___  ___  ___    9  ___
5.  100    98    96    94   ___  ___   86  ___  ___
6.  ___   ___   ___    25    30    35  ___  ___  ___
7.    7    14    21   ___  ___  ___   49  ___
8.   25    50   ___   100  ___  ___  175  ___  ___
9.   99    96    93    90   ___  ___  ___   78  ___
10.  88    84    80   ___  ___  ___   60  ___
```

Take the base word and add an ending to each one. Make sure it makes sense. Read your words to an adult.

-ed   -er   -est   -able   -ible   -or   -ion   -tion

-ly   -y   -ment   -ness   -ful   -less   -ing

Remember: Base Word + Suffix = New Word

1. lose _____	11. clean _____	21. harness _____
2. arrange _____	12. erase _____	22. sand _____
3. home _____	13. sweet _____	23. expect _____
4. grate _____	14. tough _____	24. direct _____
5. thought _____	15. light _____	25. invent _____
6. peace _____	16. quick _____	26. measure _____
7. reverse _____	17. value _____	27. strong _____
8. agree _____	18. notice _____	28. collect _____
9. question _____	19. wander _____	29. love _____
10. afford _____	20. brighten _____	30. suggest _____

Day 8

Draw a line to the correct ending for each sentence.

1. The teacher wrote names   was very generous to her people.
2. The girl did not want to   learn to take responsibility for what to do.
3. In the story *The Magic Beans,*   we see many travelers.
4. The queen of Tooly Town   leave her old school.
5. North America is a   is going to hit your head.
6. What did you do with   huge appetite for fish.
7. In the summertime   red handkerchief in his pocket.
8. Is a greenhouse a   on the board with chalk.
9. Sometimes you have to   very big continent.
10. The tall boy had a large,   out the secret.
11. My little sister blurted   much that he started to cry.
12. Look out! That ball   my new rollerblades?
13. Wendy and I rode our   bicycles in the Fourth of July parade.
14. My pet cat, Al, has a   place where you can grow plants?
15. The news affected him so   Jack climbed up a beanstalk.

Rain and snow provide water for our earth. When it rains or snows, water goes into the ground, streams, rivers, and other bodies of water. Little rivers run into big rivers, and big rivers run into the oceans. The sun pulls up some of the water and forms clouds. This is called evaporation. The clouds get heavy and form rain or snow that falls back to earth. This process is called the water cycle.

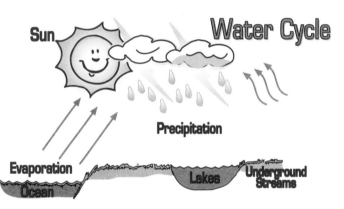

True or False. Put a T for true and an F for false.

_____ 1. All living things need water.
_____ 2. Rain and snow are part of the water cycle.
_____ 3. Water is evaporated by the sun.
_____ 4. No rivers run into the ocean.
_____ 5. Clouds make the water evaporate.
_____ 6. Another name for ocean is sea.
_____ 7. All water is good to drink.
_____ 8. People pollute the water.

How Many?

1. How many 6's are there in 18? _____
2. How many 5's are there in 25? _____
3. How many 2's are there in 8? _____
4. How many 4's are there in 20? _____
5. How many 9's are there in 18? _____
6. How many 7's are there in 21? _____
7. How many 3's are there in 12? _____
8. How many 8's are there in 32? _____
9. How many 6's are there in 24? _____
10. How many 1's are there in 70? _____
11. How many 4's are there in 16? _____
12. How many 3's are there in 15? _____

Read the sentences and mark if the underlined word is spelled right or wrong.

	Right	Wrong
EXAMPLE: Hal <u>also</u> has a new, red car.	X	
That was an <u>unnkind</u> thing to say.		X
1. <u>I'd</u> like a glass of water.		
2. Do you know where <u>theyv'e</u> been today?		
3. Be <u>carefull</u> with that knife.		
4. My mom was very <u>unhappy</u> today.		
5. What did Joan plant in her <u>gardin</u>?		
6. We looked at all the <u>babyies</u> in the hospital.		
7. Aunt Mary bottled ten pounds of <u>cherries</u>.		
8. He waved at us from the <u>window</u>.		
9. Dad bought a big <u>balluen</u> for my little sister.		
10. The deer ate <u>allmost</u> all of our bushes last winter.		
11. Have you gone <u>swimming</u> often this summer?		
12. I <u>won't</u> be going to the same school next fall.		

Read the story. Write complete sentences for your answers.

Robert and Scott are two of my very best friends. We have gone to school together since we were in kindergarten. We even go to summer camp and the recreation center together. There are many reasons why I like to be with them. Robert always lets me borrow his skateboard. He knows that if I had a skateboard, I would let him borrow it. Robert is a person you can count on, too. When we are out riding our bikes together, Scott sometimes has me ride in front while he rides behind me. He understands that the way to be a good friend is by taking turns and being fair.

1. What is it that Robert does to be a good friend?

_____

_____

2. Is Scott a fair person? Why?

_____

_____

3. List three things that the friends do together.

_____

_____

_____

4. Write a few sentences of your own about what you think makes a good friend.

_____

_____

_____

_____

_____

_____

Story Problems.

1. Nancy weighs 43 pounds. Janet weighs 34 pounds. How many pounds do they weigh together? _____

2. Bill threw 259 balls, and Kirk only threw 137. How many more balls did Bill throw than Kirk? _____

3. Jake collected 694 marbles. Joyce collected 966. How many fewer marbles did Jake collect than Joyce? _____

4. Mary Ann had a stack of 42 cards. She wants to divide them into 6 stacks. How many will she have in each stack? _____

5. Ralph had 4 stacks of cookies, with 4 in each stack. How many cookies does he have in all? _____

Say these words and circle the number that tells how many syllables you hear.

1. ambulance	2. tiger	3. banana	4. saddle	5. magnet	6. watermelon	7. shoe
1 2 3 4	1 2 3 4	1 2 3 4	1 2 3 4	1 2 3 4	1 2 3 4	1 2 3 4
8. radio	9. necklace	10. brush	11. dragon	12. seven	13. book	14. tulip
1 2 3 4	1 2 3 4	1 2 3 4	1 2 3 4	1 2 3 4	1 2 3 4	1 2 3 4
15. butterfly	16. hammer	17. telephone	18. torch	19. rhinoceros	20. paper	21. lemonade
1 2 3 4	1 2 3 4	1 2 3 4	1 2 3 4	1 2 3 4	1 2 3 4	1 2 3 4
22. shark	23. blanket	24. fifty	25. camel	26. dart	27. popsicles	28. binoculars
1 2 3 4	1 2 3 4	1 2 3 4	1 2 3 4	1 2 3 4	1 2 3 4	1 2 3 4

Day 10

Circle the letter to answer the question and then divide the underlined words into syllables.

1. A <u>chipmunk</u> is about the size of a gerbil.
   Chipmunk means   a. **plant**   b. **bug**   c. **animal**
2. Richard <u>collects</u> stamps.
   Collect means   a. **save**   b. **give away**   c. **licks**
3. The cows will <u>produce</u> lots of milk this summer.
   Produce means   a. **drink**   b. **eat**   c. **give**
4. Anna had lots of <u>spangles</u> on her party dress.
   Spangles means   a. **bright objects**   b. **dull objects**   c. **paper**
5. The tires on the car left an <u>imprint</u> on the grass.
   Imprint means   a. **mark**   b. **oil**   c. **water**
6. We saw a <u>splendid</u> movie last night.
   Splendid means   a. **bad**   b. **loud**   c. **wonderful**
7. Marsha has a beautiful <u>silver</u> watch.
   Silver means   a. **paint**   b. **metal**   c. **gold**
8. Some baby <u>goslings</u> were in our pond.
   Goslings are   a. **young geese**   b. **old geese**   c. **young chickens**

How Do Seeds Grow?
Write down the conditions that are necessary for seeds to germinate and grow.

Multiply.

```
   6       5       9       9       3       8       9       6
  x4      x2      x7      x0      x5      x4      x6      x5
```

1 x 7 = _____   6 x 8 = _____   3 x 8 = _____

3 x 2 = _____   2 x 7 = _____   7 x 7 = _____

4 x 4 = _____   8 x 8 = _____   1 x 9 = _____

5 x 9 = _____   3 x 3 = _____   5 x 5 = _____

```
   1       9       6       0       9       2       5       0
  x8      x2      x6      x7      x9      x2      x5      x0
```

Make each underlined word mean more than one (plural) and write it in the blank.

EXAMPLE:

1. One baby <u>calf</u>, plus one more, makes two baby _calves_ .

2. The <u>wolf</u> howled until two _____ howled with him.

3. She put a book on a <u>shelf</u> and put all the other books on the rest

of the _____.

4. The blacksmith put a horseshoe on the horse's <u>hoof</u> and then he

put the others on the rest of the _____.

5. The <u>child</u> played alone, until the other _____ came.

6. He left his <u>wife</u> with all the other _____ at the PTA meeting.

Day 11

Choose a word from the Word Bank that fits each meaning. Then write it in the puzzle.

Down

2. very, very sad
4. spin around and around
6. making something look larger
8. very sure of something
10. not better

Across

1. need to do it right now
3. send back to the store
5. take care of the sick
7. to go after
9. the earth

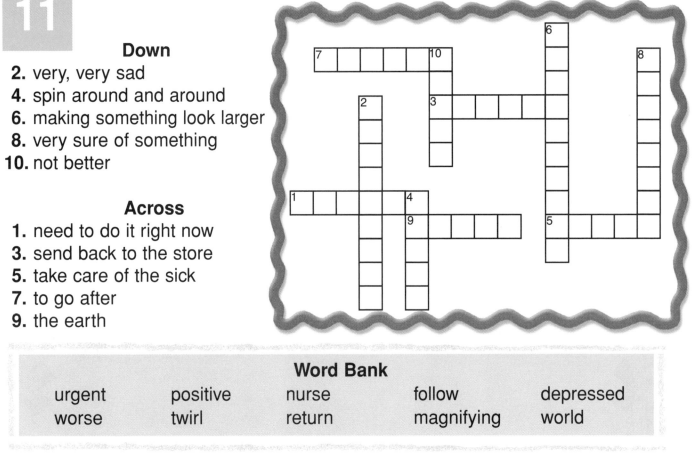

Word Bank

urgent	positive	nurse	follow	depressed
worse	twirl	return	magnifying	world

Inventions

The telephone was invented in 1876; the first widely sold lightbulb was invented in 1879. The handheld camera was invented in 1888 and the tractor in 1900. What would you like to invent that could be important to yourself and others? Think of something you might invent in the future. Either write about or draw a picture of your invention, or both.

Use the graph to answer the questions.

Ms. Fran has many friends. She sends them letters each week. Mark the answers to the questions on the graph.
(Monday is done for you.)
Each letter shown stands for four letters.

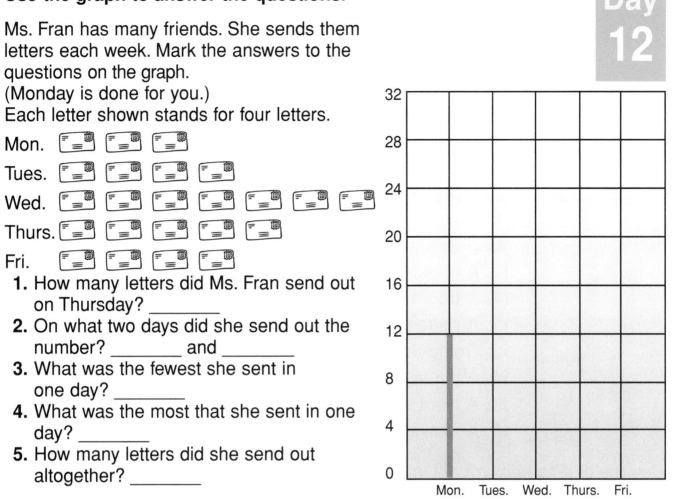

Mon.
Tues.
Wed.
Thurs.
Fri.

32
28
24
20
16
12
8
4
0

Mon. Tues. Wed. Thurs. Fri.

1. How many letters did Ms. Fran send out on Thursday? _____
2. On what two days did she send out the number? _____ and _____
3. What was the fewest she sent in one day? _____
4. What was the most that she sent in one day? _____
5. How many letters did she send out altogether? _____

Similarities and Differences. Look at each pair of words. Write down at least one way they are alike and at least one way they are different.

1. leopard and cheetah _____

_____

_____

2. typewriter and piano _____

_____

_____

3. cabin and tent _____

_____

_____

4. whistle and sing _____

_____

_____

Real or Make-Believe. Write <u>M</u> for make-believe and <u>R</u> for real.

_____ **1.** A pumpkin growing on a vine in a field.

_____ **2.** A fireman saving a kitten from a tree.

_____ **3.** An elephant that can fly in a circus.

_____ **4.** A cow that can give chocolate milk.

_____ **5.** A family taking a summer vacation.

_____ **6.** A chicken that lays golden eggs.

_____ **7.** A brother and sister working together.

_____ **8.** Five children going to a movie in the afternoon.

_____ **9.** Buckets of paint turning the sky many colors.

_____ **10.** A ghost turning a frog into a king.

_____ **11.** A tree being blown over by the wind.

_____ **12.** A rainbow bridge to the moon.

_____ **13.** Going for a boat ride down the Mississippi.

_____ **14.** A big tree growing overnight.

_____ **15.** A giant who eats children.

_____ **16.** A man who is seven-and-a-half feet tall.

Use the clue to help you fill in the missing letters. <u>Hint:</u> Use vowels.

1. to do something many times   __ft__n

2. a sea animal with eight legs   __ct__p__s

3. a reptile that lives in a swamp   cr__c__d__l__

4. a very small house   c__tt__ge

5. something to keep the rain off   __mbr__ll__

6. twelve things   d__z__n

7. a tree or the inner part of your hand   p__lm

8. two things that are different   __pp__s__t__

9. a place that has little rain   d__s__rt

10. you can put this on a Christmas tree   __rn__m__nt

11. a dessert made with eggs   c__st__rd

12. to stop something from happening   pr__v__nt

13. go away   d__s__pp__ __r

14. to say you are sorry   __p__l__g__z__

15. something that breaks easily   fr__g__l__

16. something not finished   __nc__mpl__t__

Use what you know about trading and regrouping to solve these problems. Use the place-value charts to help you.

EXAMPLE:

1. 7̶0̶3̶ (6 9 13)
   - 289
   ─────
   414

a.
H	T	O
6	10	13

b. (circled)
H	T	O
6	9	13

c.
H	T	O
5	9	10

2. 924
   - 369

a.
H	T	O
8	11	14

b.
H	T	O
9	11	10

c.
H	T	O
8	10	14

3. 900
   - 576

a.
H	T	O
8	9	10

b.
H	T	O
9	11	10

c.
H	T	O
8	10	14

4. 661
   - 287

a.
H	T	O
5	16	11

b.
H	T	O
5	15	11

c.
H	T	O
6	6	11

Which two words make up each contraction, or what contraction comes from the two words?

1. Write the contractions for these words.

we are _____   was not _____

were not _____   would not _____

2. Write the two words in these contractions.

they've _____   shouldn't _____

they'll _____   I'd _____

3. Write the contractions for these words.

he is _____   she is _____

he has _____   she has _____

4. Write the contractions for these words.

let us _____   will not _____

does not _____   we have _____

Read the directions in the box. Draw a line under the answer to each question.

1. What do the directions tell you how to make?

    a. oatmeal

    b. instant oatmeal

    c. cold cereal

2. What is the first step?

    a. turn microwave on

    b. empty package into bowl

    c. stir well to mix

3. What things do you need?

    oatmeal package, pan, water or milk, spoon, flour, sugar

4. How long should it take you to make this?

    a. a few seconds   **b.** a few minutes   **c.** 30 minutes

5. What would happen if you skipped step 2?

    a. too long to cook   **b.** dry, hot cereal   **c.** nothing

> **Instant Oatmeal**
> **1.** Empty package into microwaveable bowl.
> **2.** Add 2/3 cup water or milk and stir.
> **3.** Microwave on high 1-2 minutes; stir.
> **4.** Put milk and sugar on top.
> **5.** Eat with a spoon.
> **6.** Clean up.

Add a prefix to the words in the blanks. Use <u>re</u>- or <u>un</u>-.

1. Please _____move your shoes before you come in.

2. We will have to _____build our house.

3. He was very _____kind to me.

4. I would like to _____ join that club.

5. That was an _____usual movie.

6. We have to _____make the cake.

7. Did you feel like you were treated _____fairly?

8. The children will _____turn on Saturday.

9. That was an _____common rainstorm.

10. You will have to _____wrap that gift.

11. Please _____write this paper.

12. Why were you _____happy?

Practice finding the differences.

EX. 5 10 6̶0̶3 - 240 363	300 - 130	510 - 250	804 - 163	905 - 662	404 - 142

EX. 4 9 10 5̶0̶0̶ - 246 254	623 - 257	771 - 704	900 - 156	435 - 297	500 - 297

EX. 8 14 10 $9̶.5̶0̶ - 6.75 $2.75	$5.00 - 1.62	$6.15 - 4.38	$10.32 - 7.75	$4.06 - 1.67	$1.00 - .67

Write, in cursive, a sentence for each of the <u>-es</u> words in the box.

hooves shelves wolves lives leaves scarves wives knives	1. _____ _____ 2. _____ _____ 3. _____ _____ 4. _____ _____ 5. _____

6. _____

7. _____

8. _____

Look at this table of contents and answer the questions.

1. What chapters should you read to learn how to write a story?

   _____, _____

2. On what page should you start reading to learn about commas? _____

3. How many chapters does this table of contents show? _____

4. On which page would you find information on describing what something looks like? _____

5. In what chapter could you find out how to use a telephone? _____

6. Which chapter might tell you how to make a paper airplane? _____

Table of Contents

Read the paragraph and add the correct punctuation.

Where did you go yesterday Tanner asked Denise I went to the fair she told him I will draw a picture of it for you She then told him about the watermelon-eating contest and the blue ribbon she won She told him about seeing pigs and prize-winning sheep It sounds like you had a fun day Denise I wish I had been with you said Tanner.

Now draw a picture of something else Denise may have seen at the fair.

Read and solve the problems.

1. James planted 5 corn seeds in each of 9 holes. How many seeds did he plant?

_____ x _____ = _____

2. Betty has the same number of nickels as she has dimes. She has $1.80 worth of dimes. How many nickels does she have? _____
She has $ ____.____ in nickels.

3. There were 95 children on the bus. Ten got off at the first stop. Twenty-two got off at the second stop. How many are left on the bus? _____

4. Judy went to a book sale. In 3 days she bought 24 books. She bought the same number each time she went. How many did she buy each day?

_____

5. Sue babysat four times last week. She made $4 one night, $5.25 on two different nights, and $6.40 on the fourth night. How much did Sue make last week babysitting? _____

6. Allen picked fruit for a farmer last summer. He picked 16 bushels of peaches, 14 bushels of apples, and 18 bushels of pears. How much fruit did Allen pick? _____

Write the titles of these books correctly. <u>Remember</u>: the first, last, and all important words need to begin with a capital letter. Write in cursive.

1. nate the great _____

2. katy and the big snow _____

3. claude the dog_____

4. emma's dragon hunt _____

5. the legend of the bluebonnet _____

6. the seashore story _____

7. soup for the king _____

8. the storm book _____

9. frog and toad together_____

10. a bear called paddington_____

Finish writing this story.

> The group of hikers did not know how long it had been since anyone had seen Don. "I know he was here just a little while ago," said Fred. Fred had said that two hours ago. There were already search parties out looking for Don.
>
> "Don is a good hiker and should be able to find his way down the mountain," his father was saying. "But maybe he has been hurt," replied Don's friend, Craig.

_____

_____

_____

_____

_____

_____

_____

Try making a comparison with nature or something else.

EXAMPLE: The first daffodils were as yellow as _____ *lemons* _____.

1. The piano keys were as white as _____.

2. The new leaves on the trees in spring are as green as_____.

3. My new sweater was as blue as the summer _____.

4. That horse is as black as a dark _____.

5. The fireworks were as bright as the _____.

6. Her eyes were as green as the _____.

7. The balloons reminded me of a bunch of _____.

8. That house was as tall as a steep _____.

9. The mud between my toes was as brown as _____.

10. The sunset was as red and orange as _____.

11. The rings on her fingers sparkled like _____.

12. The bread we were trying to eat was as hard as a _____.

13. I was so tired, my pillow felt as soft as a _____.

14. The wind was as gentle as _____.

Count the money.

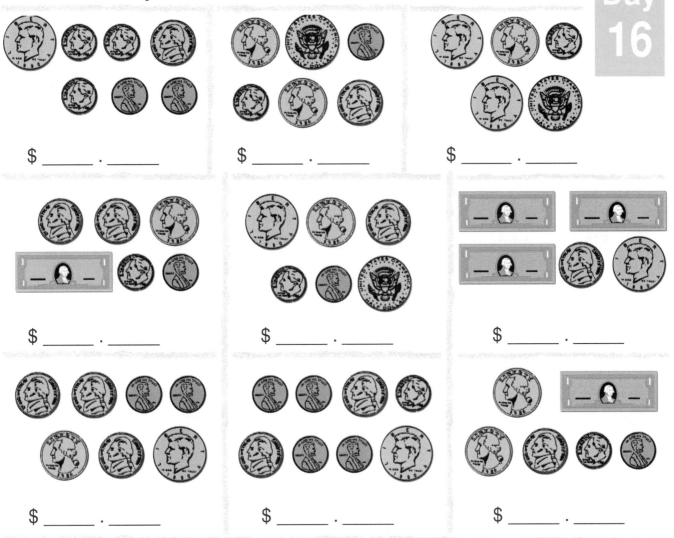

$ _____ . _____ $ _____ . _____ $ _____ . _____

$ _____ . _____ $ _____ . _____ $ _____ . _____

$ _____ . _____ $ _____ . _____ $ _____ . _____

The main idea tells what a story is all about. Usually, one sentence tells the main idea. Find the sentence in the story that tells the main idea and underline it.

1. Penny Puppy eats strange snacks. She likes to chew on old socks, making holes in them. She eats pussy willows and catnip leaves. Her favorite snack is bug bars. However, whenever you see Penny Puppy, she will always have a snack bone necklace around her neck.

2. Oliver Owl tries to teach Ollie Owl how to fly, but Ollie has a difficult time learning. Oliver tells Ollie to perch on the highest branch of the tallest tree. "Then jump and flap your little wings as hard as you can!" he says. Ollie tries but just somersaults all the way down. Oliver just barely catches Ollie on the last branch. Oliver decides he was not meant to teach little owls how to fly!

Number each sentence in the correct order.

How to Make a Beanbag

_____ Fill the sock up with beans.

_____ Get a friend to play with you.

_____ Find an old sock that you won't be using for anything else.

_____ Make up a fun game to be played with a beanbag and a friend.

_____ Check out the beanbag by tossing and catching it a few times.

_____ Check the sock to make sure it doesn't have any holes in it.

_____ Tie the sock with a knot in the end or with a strong piece of string.

Draw and color the other half of the picture.

Use the information given on meters and kilometers to help you solve the problems.

1 meter = 100 centimeters	1 kilometer = 1,000 meters
cm = centimeter m = meter	km = kilometer

Choose a unit so the answers seem reasonable.

1. Randy is 150 _____ tall.

2. Jane's room is 5 _____ wide.

3. Whitney's hand is 14 _____ long and 5 _____ wide.

4. The distance from Florida to Texas is 1,150 _____.

5. The flagpole at the post office is 46 _____ tall.

6. I can touch the wall 163 _____ high.

7. Mr. Hobbs drove his car 84 _____ the first hour.

8. Joyce's room is about 6 _____ wide.

9. The door is about 2 _____ high.

10. Jack and Jill walked approximately 3 _____ in 30 minutes.

11. The fence around Mark's yard is 4 _____ tall.

Writers sometimes use words that stand for other words. They call them "word referents." Read each sentence. Circle the word that the underlined word stands for.

EXAMPLE:

1. Betty has a (computer.) She keeps <u>it</u> on her desk.

2. Dora said, "<u>I</u> have to go home now to visit <u>my</u> grandmother."

3. Bill asked Juan if <u>he</u> was going to play baseball this year.

4. Jack and Jean both collect seashells. Sometimes <u>they</u> trade with one another.

5. Rachel plays the violin, and sometimes <u>she</u> sings, too.

6. When the big, gray dog saw the cat, <u>he</u> barked and growled.

7. Our school bus is always crowded and <u>it</u> is usually very noisy, too.

8. Mom might let us go sledding today. We might get <u>her</u> to drive us to the hill at the park.

Read the story and answer the questions.

Denise has a dog named Pocket. Pocket hates to take a bath. Whenever he hears water running, Pocket runs outside and hides in the playhouse. Last week, Denise decided Pocket had to have a bath. Denise took a round tub out on the lawn and started to fill it with warm water. When the tub was ready, Denise called her dog. "Come here, Pocket. It's time for your bath."

1. Do you think Pocket will come to Denise? Why or why not?

_____

_____

_____

2. Where do you think Denise will find Pocket? Why?

_____

_____

_____

3. What would you do if you had a dog like Pocket?

_____

_____

_____

Write the spelling words that fit in each shape.

straight	neighbor	through	friend	message
breakfast	person	spread	double	libraries

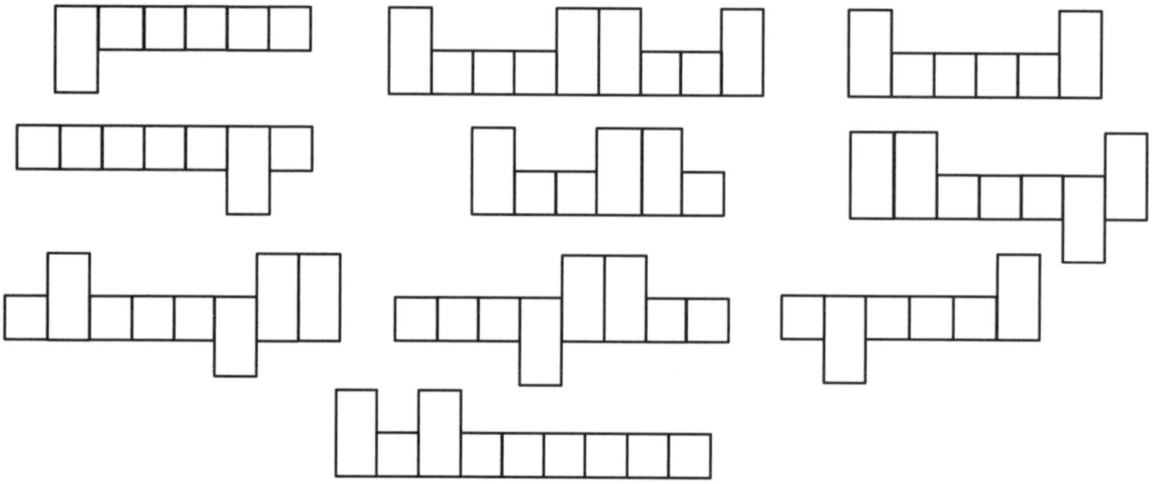

Find the missing factors. One factor and the product are given to you.

1. ____ X 3 = 6	____ X 6 = 30	4 X ____ =16	____ X 2 = 10
2. 3 X ____ = 18	7 X ____ = 14	____ X 9 = 18	____ X 10 = 20
3. ____ X 5 = 5	12 X ____ = 12	____ X 8 = 24	6 X ____ = 36
4. 1 X ____ = 9	4 X ____ = 28	9 X ____ = 81	5 X ____ = 50
5. 3 X ____ = 21	____ X 5 = 25	____ X 7 = 49	3 X ____ = 9
6. ____ X 2 = 4	9 X ____ = 36	8 X ____ = 72	5 X ____ = 35
7. 5 X ____ = 45	2 X ____ = 30	10 X ____ = 50	7 X ____ = 42
8. 12 X ____ = 36	3 X ____ = 27	6 X ____ = 60	____ X 1 = 10

The words in each row go together in some way. Write two more words to go with them.

EXAMPLE:

1. robin, owl, pigeon   *quail*   *pheasant*

2. peaches, apples, pears   _____   _____

3. spoon, bowl, cup   _____   _____

4. lake, pond, river   _____   _____

5. branch, sticks, wood   _____   _____

6. lemonade, water, milk   _____   _____

7. dollar, dime, penny   _____   _____

8. carrot, celery, pears   _____   _____

9. dress, shoes, skirt   _____   _____

10. tennis, golf, racquetball   _____   _____

Fill in the blanks. Use <u>plant</u>, <u>heat</u>, <u>sunlight</u>, <u>plants</u>, <u>Earth</u>, <u>sunlight</u>, <u>oxygen.</u>

Sunlight is very important to our planet, _____. It provides us with food, oxygen, and _____. Most of our food comes from _____ life. _____ also give off the _____ we breathe. Without _____, plants would die, and we would not have food or air. The _____ also heats the earth. Without it, we would freeze to death.

1. What is the topic?

   a. food

   b. sunlight

   c. oxygen

   d. plants

2. What is the main idea?

   a. Sunlight is important to the earth.

   b. Sunlight heats plants.

   c. People would freeze without sunlight.

   d. Sunlight hurts your eyes.

Words that mean about the same are called synonyms. Write, in cursive, a synonym from the box below for the words listed.

Ex. **easy** — *simple*	shout	change
also	jacket	home
gift	car	complete
close	gem	join
shy	penny	mistake
wet	rug	argument
rich	couch	scared

~~simple~~	yell	present	timid	house	shut	afraid
finish	jewel	sofa	coat	error	automobile	moist
too	carpet	wealthy	alter	cent	connect	dispute

12	8	6	15	6	13	14	8
- 8	+ 9	x 4	- 9	x 7	- 5	+ 7	x 6

19	46	75	38	44	83	57	37
+ 39	- 28	- 39	+ 17	- 15	- 47	+ 34	+ 36

8	4	3	27	40	35	65	6
x 4	x 7	x 9	+ 19	- 8	+ 44	- 59	x 9

804	132	176	921	608	304	657	813
- 238	- 78	+ 394	+ 496	- 239	- 127	- 589	- 738

Pretend you were walking in a park last night and saw a spaceship land. Write a paragraph about it. How did it look? How did it make you feel? Did anyone else see it? Did you see or speak to anyone or anything?

Read the story carefully. Watch for word meanings.

Matt lives in a large city with his grandparents. The building that he and his grandparents live in is very tall and has different sets of rooms for each family that lives there. This building is called an apartment. In this neighborhood, all of the buildings are fairly tall and close together. People do not have to go far to get things in this urban area. Matt's cousin, Damon, lives in a small, rural, country community. He has a large backyard to play in instead of a park like Matt. There is a lot of space between the houses where Damon lives. Both Matt's and Damon's neighborhoods have schools, hospitals, stores, and other places people need.

Write down a meaning for the following words:

1. community _____

_____

2. apartment _____

_____

3. rural area _____

_____

Write a short paragraph about your home and community.

Fractions. Divide the shapes according to the fraction asked for.

EXAMPLE:

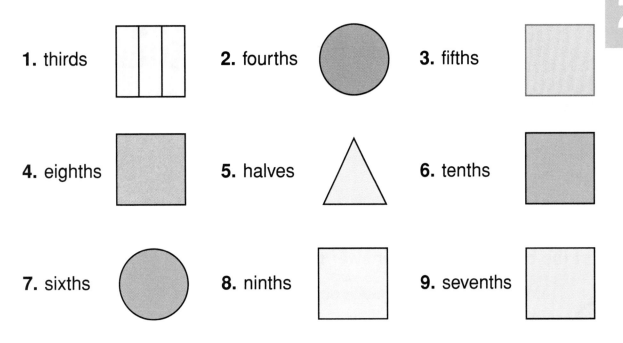

1. thirds   2. fourths   3. fifths

4. eighths   5. halves   6. tenths

7. sixths   8. ninths   9. sevenths

10. Start with a paper strip ⬚ Fold it once. Fold it again. Fold it once more. Before you unfold it, think to yourself, "How do the folds divide the paper, and how many equal parts do I have?" Now check to see if you are right.

Write the words under the correct word category.

buttermilk
airplane
snowstorm
selection
replanted
overweight
sleepless
peaceful
happiness
football
daylight
eyesight
unpacked
sandalwood

Compound words	Words with prefixes or suffixes

Day 20

It's Time Again!

1. Write the times.

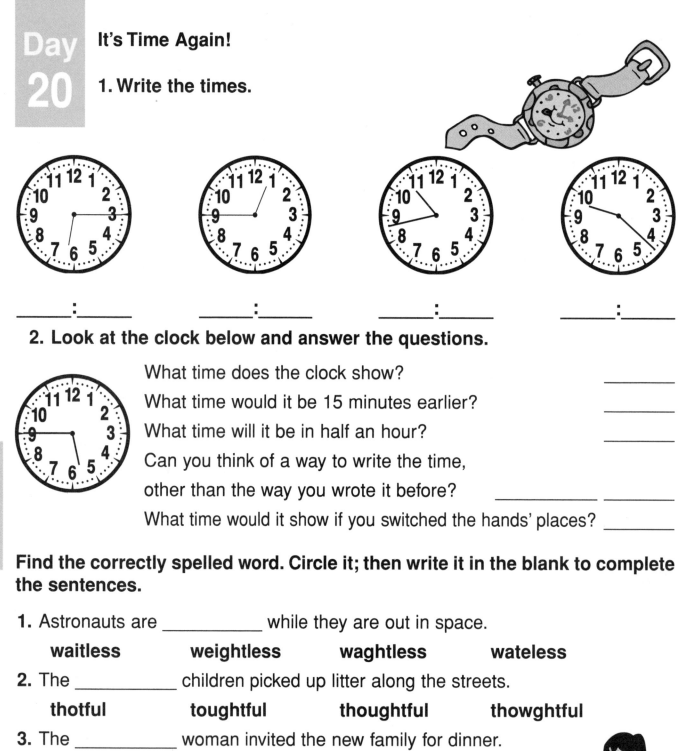

_____:_____   _____:_____   _____:_____   _____:_____

2. Look at the clock below and answer the questions.

What time does the clock show? _____

What time would it be 15 minutes earlier? _____

What time will it be in half an hour? _____

Can you think of a way to write the time,

other than the way you wrote it before? _____ _____

What time would it show if you switched the hands' places? _____

Find the correctly spelled word. Circle it; then write it in the blank to complete the sentences.

1. Astronauts are _____ while they are out in space.

    waitless   **weightless**   **waghtless**   **wateless**

2. The _____ children picked up litter along the streets.

    thotful   **toughtful**   **thoughtful**   **thowghtful**

3. The _____ woman invited the new family for dinner.

    neighborly   **neighborlie**   **naborly**   **knaborly**

4. We need to remember to keep our doctor's _____.

    apointment   **apowntment**   **appointment**

5. Make some _____ of this, please.

    copyes   **copies**   **copeis**   **coppies**

6. This box is a lot _____ than the other one was.

    emptyer   **emptier**   **emptys**   **emptiest**

Words to Sound, Read, and Spell

cased	clock	content	dancer	disapproving
caterpillar	close	contest	dangerous	discouraged
cattle	closer	contraption	dared	discover
caught	closet	convenient	darkness	discovered
cavern	closing	corner	darted	disgrace
cement	clothes	cost	darting	dissolved
center	cloud	costume	daughter	doctor
certainly	clown	cottage	deadly	dodged
chance	clubhouse	cotton	dealt	doesn't
change	cluck	could	dearly	dollars
characters	clue	couldn't	debating	dolphins
charcoal	clues	count	decided	donation
chart	clump	countdown	declared	doorknob
chased	clung	counter	decoding	doorstep
cheeks	clutched	country	deepening	double
cheered	coach	couple	deeply	doubt
cheerfully	coast	courage	defeat	doubtful
cheese	coaster	courageous	defeated	dough
chest	cobbled	course	degree	downstairs
chewed	coconut	courting	delicious	dozen
chicken	code	courtyard	delight	drift
chief	coin	cousin	deliver	driven
childhood	cold	covered	demanded	dropped
children	colder	crafty	department	druggist
chimney	coldness	crashed	depends	dugout
chipped	college	crawled	describes	during
chisel	colors	cream	desert	dusk
choose	columns	creature	deserves	duty
chopsticks	comes	cricket	design	eager
chorus	comet	crispy	desires	early
chose	comfort	croaking	despair	earn
chunks	comfortable	crouched	desperate	earth
chunky	comical	crown	desperately	easier
circus	coming	crumble	dessert	easily
citizens	command	crushed	destroy	eaten
clasped	commands	crying	detectives	echoes
class	communicate	curious	diamond	edge
claw	companies	curled	diary	eighth
clay	company	curls	dictionary	either
clean	compartment	current	different	elephants
cleaner	complained	curve	dime	elevator
clever	completely	custard	dimmed	eleven
click	concert	custom	dinner	embarrassed
climb	condensed	dabbled	direction	enable
climbed	confused	dainty	director	endless
cloak	contain	danced	disappointed	enemy

Words to Sound, Read, and Spell

enforce	faith	floating	gathered	groans
engines	fallen	flocking	gazed	groom
enjoyed	falling	footbridge	gear	groomed
enough	famous	footprints	generous	grooming
equipment	fancy	forbidden	gentle	grouchy
escalator	fantastic	force	gentleman	grumpy
escape	faraway (adj.)	forepaws	gently	guest
especially	farther	forever	germ	guide
evening	fault	forgetting	giant	guitar
everybody	favor	forgotten	gigantic	gulp
everyday (adj.)	favorite	forth	gingerbread	gulped
everyone	fear	fortune	giraffes	gum
everything	fellow	forward	give	guppies
everywhere	fern	fossil	given	gym
exactly	fetch	fountain	giving	hailstorms
examining	fever	fourteen	glanced	ham
excellent	fiction	fourth	glared	hammer
except	fiddle	frantically	gleaming	hammering
excited	field	frayed	glimmer	handful
excitedly	fiery	freezer	glimmering	handle
excitement	fifteen	friendliness	glimpse	handshake
exclaims	fifty	fright	glint	handsome
exercises	fighters	frightened	glisten	handwriting
exhaled	figures	frisky	glittered	happened
exhausted	finally	froggy	gnaw	happily
exits	fingermarks	frolicked	golden	happiness
expect	fingerprints	frowned	good-natured	harm
expected	finish	froze	goodness	harness
expecting	finished	frozen	goose pimples	harvested
experiment	firm	frying	gotten	haunted
expert	firmly	fur-covered	graceful	haven't
experts	flakes	furious	gracefully	hayloft
explain	flaming	furniture	gracious	hazel
explained	flapjacks	further	granite	headache
explosion	flapped	future	grant	headed
extra	flared	fuzzy	grated	health
eyebrows	flashlight	gain	gratefully	healthier
factory	flavor	gallons	gravy	healthy
faded	flaw	gallop	grin	heap
failure	flick	garage	grinned	heaps
faint	flights	garden	grip	heavens
fainted	flippers	gasped	groaned	heavily

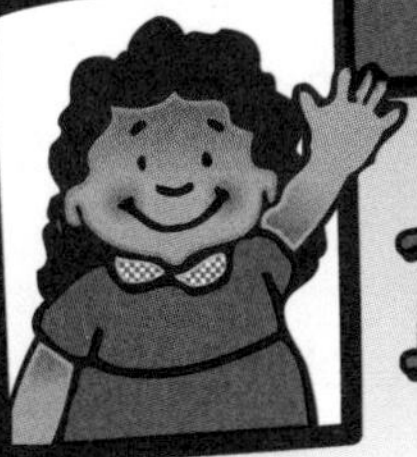

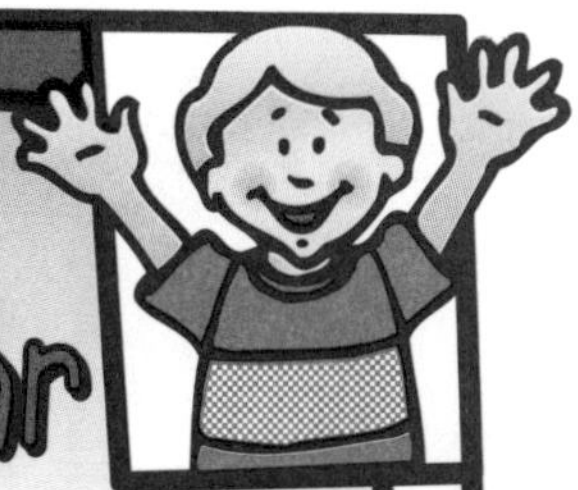

Summer Bridge Activities™

Incentive Contract Calendar

Month _____

My parents and I decided that if I complete 15 days of
Summer Bridge Activities™ and read _____ minutes a day,
my incentive/reward will be:

_____

Child's Signature _____
Parent's Signature _____

Day 1   📖 ⭐ ——   Day 8   📖 ⭐ ——

Day 2   📖 ⭐ ——   Day 9   📖 ⭐ ——

Day 3   📖 ⭐ ——   Day 10   📖 ⭐ ——

Day 4   📖 ⭐ ——   Day 11   📖 ⭐ ——

Day 5   📖 ⭐ ——   Day 12   📖 ⭐ ——

Day 6   📖 ⭐ ——   Day 13   📖 ⭐ ——

Day 7   📖 ⭐ ——   Day 14   📖 ⭐ ——

   Day 15   📖 ⭐ ——

Child: Color the ⭐ for daily activities completed.
Color the 📖 for daily reading completed.

Parent: Initial the _____ for daily activities and reading
your child completes.

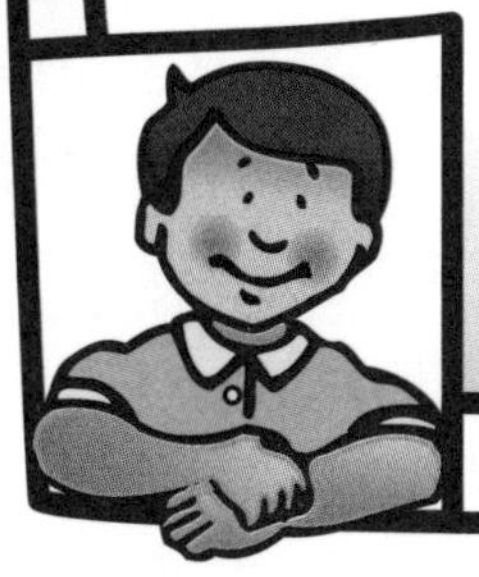

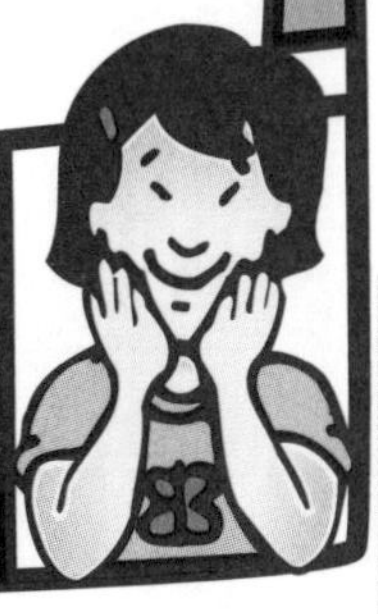

Discover Something New!

Fun Activity Ideas to Go Along with the Third Section!

1 Put on a play using old clothes as costumes.

 2 Make a game of practicing times tables.

3 Use a block of ice to cool off and slide down a grassy hill.

4 Make snow cones with crushed ice and Kool-Aid.

5 Surprise an elderly neighbor by weeding his/her garden.

6 Create a family symphony with bottles, pans, and rubber bands.

 7 Write a letter to a relative.

 8 Browse for school clothes. Calculate the money needed for purchases.

 9 Finger-paint—outside.

 10 Lie on the grass and pick designs out of the clouds.

11 Read some library books about birds.

 **12** Make some 3-D art using feathers, twigs, etc.

 13 Paint the sidewalk with water.

 14 Collect sticks and mud—then build a bird's nest.

 15 Go to the woods or lake for for an early morning "bird watch."

Counting Change.

Spent	Gave clerk	How much change?
EXAMPLE: $1.35	$1.50	$.15
$2.50	$5.00	
$.95	$1.00	
$1.80	$2.00	
$6.42	$10.00	

Spent	Gave clerk	How much change?
$9.35	$20.00	
$5.55	$6.00	
$13.95	$20.00	
$85.00	$100.00	
$100.60	$105.00	

Have you seen a parade this summer? If so, write about it. If not, make up a story about a circus parade. Give it a title. Write in cursive.

_____

_____

_____

_____

_____

_____

_____

_____

_____

_____

_____

81

Fill in the blanks.

1. Be sure to put some money in the _____.
2. The _____ on his bike was broken.
3. For good eyesight and strong teeth, we need plenty of _____.
4. _____ is made from milk.
5. The _____ did not like his speech.
6. We also need _____ to help us stay healthy.
7. Do you ever go to the _____ center?
8. My family took a _____ to England.
9. I will _____ some oranges for my juice.
10. My _____ is to become a doctor.
11. Do you like to read tall _____ ?
12. Jim got a deep cut on his _____.
13. What _____ will you wear to the party?
14. Would it be _____ for me to become president?

Word Box

minerals
pedal
vitamins
yogurt
meter
costume
squeeze
tales
possible
public
flight
ambition
community
thigh

Stressed Syllables. The "stressed" syllable is said with a little more force than the others. Circle the stressed syllable in each of the following words. Use a dictionary if you need help. In a dictionary, the stressed syllable is preceded or followed by an accent mark.

EXAMPLE: **es cape´   es ca̲pe̲**

1. doc tor
2. gar den
3. re sult
4. es ca la tor
5. con fus ing
6. com plete
7. man age
8. con tain er
9. fac to ry
10. oc ca sion
11. mess en ger
12. un til
13. li ons
14. char ac ter
15. de tec tive
16. mead ow
17. sur prise
18. daugh ter
19. at ten tion
20. rock et

Multiplication and division facts are related.

6 x 3 = 18   3 x 6 = 18   18 ÷ 6 = 3   18 ÷ 3 = 6

Use what you know to write the related facts for each problem.

5 x 3 = ___

__ x __ = ___

__ ÷ __ = ___

__ ÷ __ = ___

2. 9 x 2 = ___

__ x __ = ___

__ ÷ __ = ___

__ ÷ __ = ___

7 x 3 = ___

__ x __ = ___

__ ÷ __ = ___

__ ÷ __ = ___

4. 4 x 3 = ___

__ x __ = ___

__ ÷ __ = ___

__ ÷ __ = ___

5. 6 x 4 = ___

__ x __ = ___

__ ÷ __ = ___

__ ÷ __ = ___

4 x 8 = ___

__ x __ = ___

__ ÷ __ = ___

__ ÷ __ = ___

7. 5 x 6 = ___

__ x __ = ___

__ ÷ __ = ___

__ ÷ __ = ___

9 x 4 = ___

__ x __ = ___

__ ÷ __ = ___

__ ÷ __ = ___

Make up one of
your own.

_____ x _____ = _____

_____ x _____ = _____

_____ ÷ _____ = _____

_____ ÷ _____ = _____

Look at the first word in each row; then find the words in the row that have the same vowel sound. Circle them.
(<u>Hint</u>: They do not need to have the same vowels.)

1. noise —	joy	choose	choice	boy	mower	voice
2. wrote —	frog	both	coat	know	bought	grow
3. book —	choose	look	foot	spoon	tooth	hook
4. there —	bear	hair	share	near	bread	spare
5. large —	star	yard	scare	mark	guard	far
6. proud —	slow	crowd	now	ouch	shout	round
7. taste —	eight	white	wait	height	paint	ate
8. work —	world	store	short	word	stork	fourth

Choose the correct meaning for each word.

Now write your own meaning for these words:

1. shine
_____
_____

2. dream
_____
_____

3 different
_____
_____

4. bored
_____
_____

5. weird
_____
_____

_____stick
_____choice
_____nickel
_____neat
_____pretend
_____rug
_____waste
_____center
_____trap
_____spring
_____crack
_____quiet
_____stork
_____neighbors
_____done

1. the very middle
2. sudden, upward movement
3. to catch and hold
4. thin piece of wood
5. use foolishly
6. finished
7. floor covering
8. right to choose
9. a coin
10. small break
11. large bird
12. make-believe
13. people who live near
14. good order
15. very little noise

Number these sentences in the correct order.

_____Off to the moon went Joan!

_____Joan found an old tuna can.

_____Joan told the strange animal she
wanted a trip to the moon.

_____She washed the tuna can in the creek.

_____The animal said it would send her to
the moon if she gave it a pair of pink
rollerblades.

_____A strange animal appeared and told
her she could have a wish.

_____Joan got the rollerblades and gave
them to the strange animal.

Draw the strange animal.

Division: There are two ways of writing it.

1. 18 ÷ 3 = ____

2. 24 ÷ 4 = ____

3. 10 ÷ 2 = ____

4. 21 ÷ 3 = ____

5. 36 ÷ 4 = ____

6. 32 ÷ 8 = ____

7. 18 ÷ 3 = ____

8. 45 ÷ 5 = ____

9. 48 ÷ 6 = ____

10. 42 ÷ 7 = ____

11. 5)‾40‾

12. 9)‾36‾

13. 4)‾12‾

14. 7)‾56‾

15. 4)‾16‾

16. 6)‾36‾

17. 8)‾40‾

18. 9)‾27‾

19. 6)‾42‾

20. 7)‾35‾

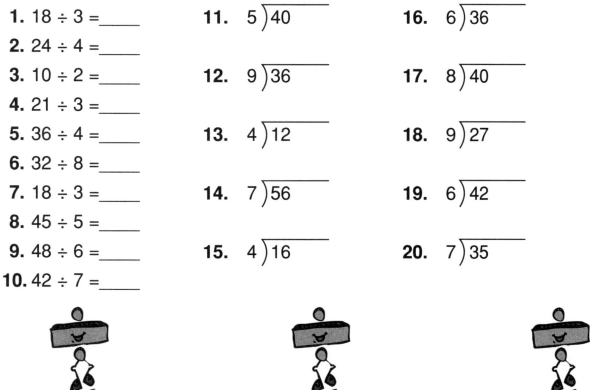

Some verbs show present tense, some show past tense, and some need a helping verb. Example: <u>go</u>, <u>give</u>, <u>take</u> = present. <u>Did</u>, <u>went</u>, <u>ran</u> = past. <u>Done</u> and <u>gone</u> need helpers. Underline the verb and then write if it is present, past, or has a helper.

EXAMPLE:

1. Mom <u>was</u> in a good mood.   *past*

2. I broke my mother's favorite vase yesterday. _____

3. Mr. Peep has given that talk many times. _____

4. I will run down the hill with you. _____

5. Her mom can take us to the ball game. _____

6. Jane did the dishes by herself. _____

7. You have gone to this school for five years. _____

8. Will you give me the money now? _____

9. Here! I will give it to you. _____

10. Let's go over to your house. _____

Batter Up, Batter Up

J. J. stepped up to the plate and waited for the pitcher to throw the ball. The pitcher pitched the ball too high, but J. J. swung at it anyway. The next ball was pitched right down the center. It was so fast, J. J. missed it completely. It was not his day. The other team's fans hooted when the pitcher struck him out. He felt bad. His feelings were hurt because some people laughed at him. He also felt he had let his teammates down. He was not a quitter, though.

Write down what you think happened or should happen next with J. J. and his team.

_____

_____

_____

_____

_____

_____

Read the words in each group. List what you think comes first, second, and third.

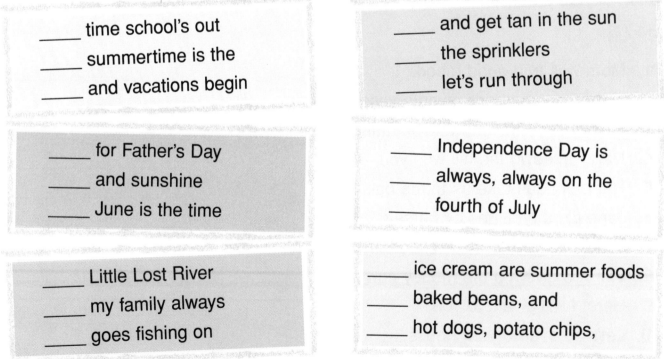

_____ time school's out
_____ summertime is the
_____ and vacations begin

_____ and get tan in the sun
_____ the sprinklers
_____ let's run through

_____ for Father's Day
_____ and sunshine
_____ June is the time

_____ Independence Day is
_____ always, always on the
_____ fourth of July

_____ Little Lost River
_____ my family always
_____ goes fishing on

_____ ice cream are summer foods
_____ baked beans, and
_____ hot dogs, potato chips,

Money Matters.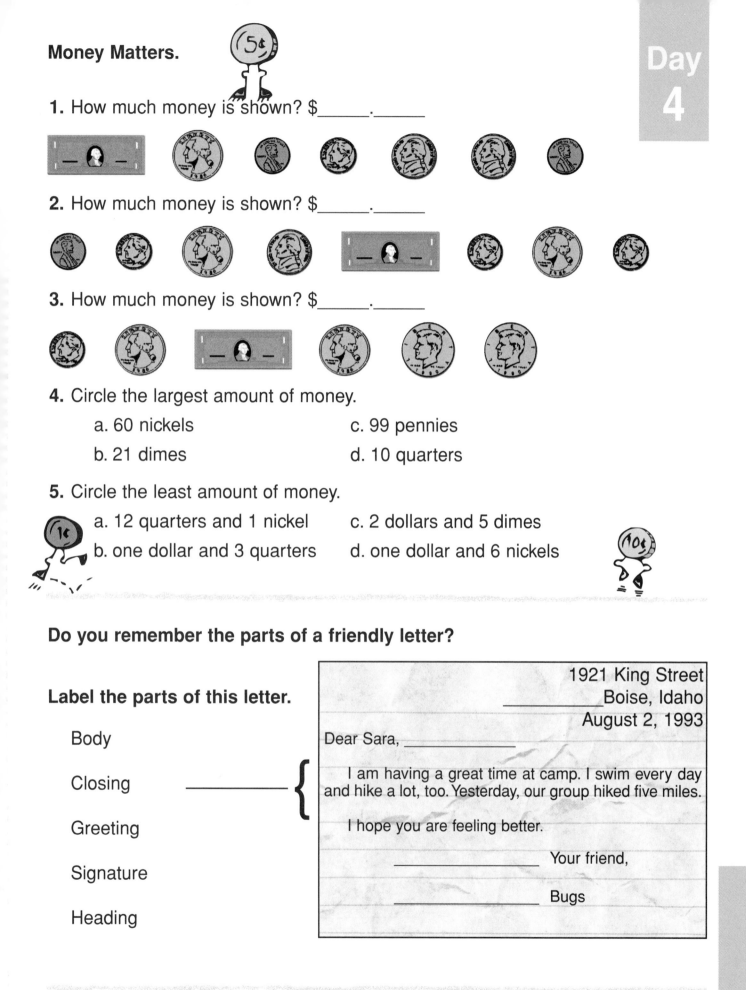

1. How much money is shown? $_____._____

2. How much money is shown? $_____._____

3. How much money is shown? $_____._____

4. Circle the largest amount of money.

    a. 60 nickels   c. 99 pennies

    b. 21 dimes   d. 10 quarters

5. Circle the least amount of money.

    a. 12 quarters and 1 nickel   c. 2 dollars and 5 dimes

    b. one dollar and 3 quarters   d. one dollar and 6 nickels

Do you remember the parts of a friendly letter?

Label the parts of this letter.

    Body

    Closing   _____ {

    Greeting

    Signature

    Heading

> 1921 King Street
> _____Boise, Idaho
> August 2, 1993
>
> Dear Sara,_____
>
>   I am having a great time at camp. I swim every day and hike a lot, too. Yesterday, our group hiked five miles.
>
>   I hope you are feeling better.
>
>   _____ Your friend,
>
>   _____ Bugs

Cause and Effect.
Read the sentences; then circle the effect, the part that tells what happened. Underline the <u>cause</u>, the part that tells why it happened.

EXAMPLE: <u>The sky became cloudy,</u> and then it started to snow.

1. The cold weather caused frost to cover the windows.
2. The falling snowflakes made my cheeks wet and cold.
3. Snow stuck to my mittens because I had made a snowman.
4. The snowman melted from the heat of the sun.
5. I played so long in the sun, I got a bad sunburn.
6. Pinnochio's nose grew longer every time he told a lie.
7. Snow White woke up when the prince kissed her.
8. The lady went to the well to get a bucket of water.
9. Our big oak tree was blown down by a strong wind.
10. Miss Mouse got very fat because she ate so much cheese.
11. The policeman gave Dad a ticket because he was going too fast.
12. We had to play in the house because it was raining hard.

Pretend this island is out in the ocean. Answer the questions about it.

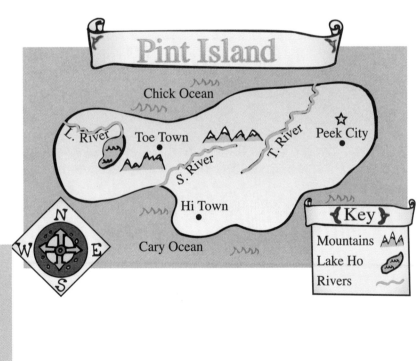

1. Which river runs into Lake Ho? _____
2. Which ocean is south of the island?_____
3. How many mountain ranges are there?_____
4. Which river is the longest? _____
5. What ocean is north of Pint Island? _____
6. What is the name of the capital city? _____
7. What direction is Hi Town from Toe Town?_____

Division.

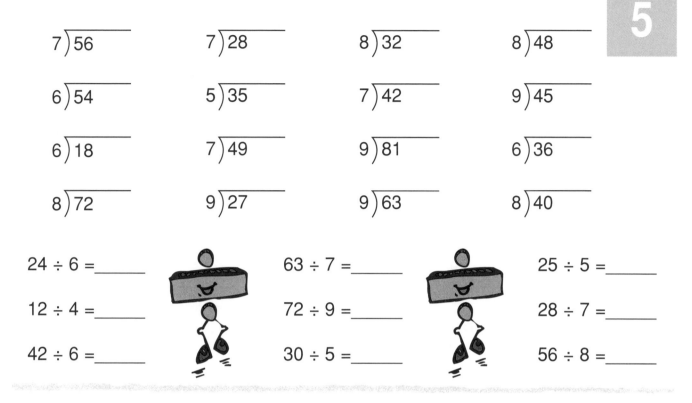

$7\overline{)56}$ $7\overline{)28}$ $8\overline{)32}$ $8\overline{)48}$

$6\overline{)54}$ $5\overline{)35}$ $7\overline{)42}$ $9\overline{)45}$

$6\overline{)18}$ $7\overline{)49}$ $9\overline{)81}$ $6\overline{)36}$

$8\overline{)72}$ $9\overline{)27}$ $9\overline{)63}$ $8\overline{)40}$

$24 \div 6 =$ _____ $63 \div 7 =$ _____ $25 \div 5 =$ _____

$12 \div 4 =$ _____ $72 \div 9 =$ _____ $28 \div 7 =$ _____

$42 \div 6 =$ _____ $30 \div 5 =$ _____ $56 \div 8 =$ _____

Circle the pronouns in the sentences. <u>Remember</u>: Pronouns take the place of a noun. There can be more than one in some sentences.

1. I told her about Val's horse.
2. This piece of cake is for him.
3. Liz invited Joe and me to the party.
4. The table is all set for us.
5. We are too late to see the first show.
6. They will be happy to come with us.
7. Ray caught two bugs, and later he freed them.
8. This pie is for you and me to eat for dessert.
9. Lisa had a hard time doing the test, but it is over now.
10. Clams and turtles have shells. They are protected by them.
11. He is Jan's best friend.
12. They have been best friends for a long time.
13. Can you find the Big Dipper in the sky?
14. My camera was broken, but Dad fixed it.

Unscramble the words and write them correctly in the blanks to complete the sentences.

1. <u>Pillows</u> are to <u>soft</u> as <u>boards</u> are to _____. **rdha**

2. <u>Oranges</u> are to <u>juicy</u> as <u>crackers</u> are to _____. **dyr**

3. <u>Braces</u> are to <u>teeth</u> as <u>glasses</u> are to _____. **esey**

4. <u>Bells</u> are to <u>ring</u> as <u>cars</u> are to _____. **nkho**

5. <u>Hear</u> is to <u>ears</u> as <u>touch</u> is to _____. **serinfg**

6. <u>Shout</u> is to <u>noise</u> as <u>whisper</u> is to _____. **uetqi**

7. <u>Star</u> is to <u>pointed</u> as <u>circle</u> is to _____. **dunor**

8. <u>Scaly</u> is to <u>fish</u> as <u>furry</u> is to _____. **ttnike**

9. <u>Ant</u> is to <u>crawl</u> as <u>frog</u> is to _____. **pael**

10. <u>Elephant</u> is to <u>large</u> as <u>mouse</u> is to _____. **malsl**

11. <u>Paint</u> is to <u>brush</u> as <u>draw</u> is to _____. **cienlp**

12. <u>Buckle</u> is to <u>belt</u> as <u>tie</u> is to _____. **laceheos**

13. <u>Bananas</u> are to <u>peel</u> as <u>eggs</u> are to _____. **cckra**

14. <u>Night</u> is to <u>dark</u> as <u>day</u> is to _____. **htgli**

Think of a story to fit the pictures. Write in the words.

Adding more than two addends.

65	22	78	51	42	87
59	46	32	26	39	32
+ 11	+ 38	+ 21	+ 26	+ 71	+ 19

54	38	39	43	37	17
19	22	71	36	46	19
+ 68	+ 46	+ 42	+ 18	+ 28	+ 12

215	325	429	742	395
463	48	330	135	205
+ 306	+ 113	+ 127	+ 173	+ 341

Read the following words. Write down how many vowels are in each word, how many vowel sounds you hear, and how many syllables there are.

	Number of vowels	Number of vowel sounds	Number of syllables
EXAMPLE: **Afraid**	3	2	2

	v	vs	syl
1. afternoon			
2. formula			
3. separated			
4. fantastic			
5. memories			
6. experience			
7. successful			

	v	vs	syl
8. education			
9. problem			
10. migrate			
11. submarine			
12. belated			
13. advertising			
14. characteristic			

Write your own ending for each sentence. Try to use more than two or three words. Write in cursive.

1. I like the flavor of _____.

2. My parents disapproved when I _____.

3. I once read a story about a boy who became a knight because he

   _____.

4. The rodeo started with _____.

5. Richard swam over to the dock to _____.

6. The kite drifted away _____.

7. The baby crawled across _____.

8. The long winter was beginning _____.

9. It was fun to watch the rabbit nibble _____.

10. The cars were piled high _____.

11. Lance won a prize for _____.

12. Do you like to play _____?

Can you put these puzzle pieces together and read the message? Don't cut them out. If you need more help, practice on a piece of scratch paper. The c and the m are already there to help you.

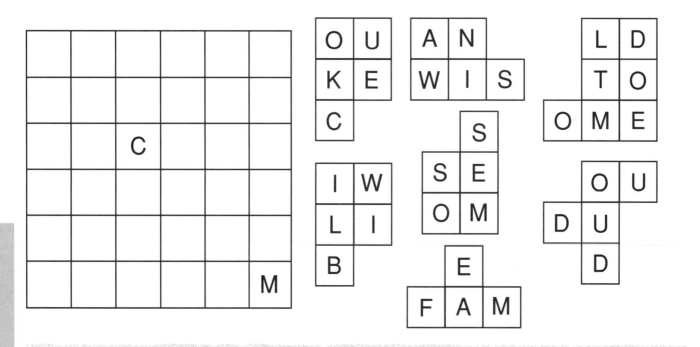

Find the products.

EXAMPLE:

```
  2
 58        42        67        66        35        23
x 3       x 8       x 5       x 3       x 6       x 3
174
```

```
 23        29        25        44        94        35
x 9       x 4       x 9       x 6       x 2       x 8
```

```
 25        21        75        68        41        63
x 4       x 6       x 4       x 3       x 7       x 2
```

```
 52        14        49        78        54        81
x 4       x 6       x 4       x 5       x 8       x 5
```

A pronoun showing ownership is a possessive pronoun, such as…

| mine | ours | yours | his | hers | theirs | its | their | my | your | mine | our |

Write six sentences in cursive. Use a possessive pronoun in each one of them.

What does the underlined phrase really mean? Circle your answer.

1. It was raining <u>cats and dogs</u>.
   a. Real cats and dogs were falling out of the sky.
   b. It was raining very hard.
   c. It wasn't raining at all.

2. The night was <u>black as coal</u>.
   a. The night was very dark.
   b. The sky was light.
   c. The night was turning into day.

3. I was so thirsty I felt like I <u>could spit cotton</u>.
   a. My mouth was very dry.
   b. I had cotton in my mouth.
   c. I did not need a drink.

4. The sun on the snow made it <u>sparkle like diamonds</u>.
   a. There were diamonds in the snow.
   b. The snow was dirty and dull.
   c. The snow was clean and shiny.

5. <u>Time flies</u> when we are having fun.
   a. Time goes quickly.
   b. Time has wings and flies like a bird.
   c. Time goes slowly.

6. The train <u>roared like a lion</u> as it went through the mountain pass.
   a. The train was quiet.
   b. The train has a voice.
   c. The train was loud and fast.

7. Andy made two <u>home runs</u> during the ball game.
   a. Andy ran home.
   b. Andy ran around all the bases and scored.
   c. Andy got out.

8. My sister is as <u>gentle as a lamb</u> with sick people.
   a. My sister is soft.
   b. My sister doesn't like sick people.
   c. My sister is kind to sick people.

Find the quotients and the remainders.

EXAMPLE:

6 R 2
4) 26

3) 14   5) 39   3) 16   3) 23

2) 19   6) 29   4) 21   5) 36   4) 18

5) 34   4) 22   5) 42   4) 33   5) 27

2) 84   3) 60   3) 51   4) 96   5) 80

3) 93   4) 76   2) 90   4) 44   4) 72

2) 50   3) 84   3) 78   4) 56   4) 68

Cursive writing review. School starts soon, so remember to…

1. Make each letter smooth and clear.
2. Space letters evenly.
3. Make each letter the correct shape and size.
4. Make each letter touch the line correctly.
5. Make your letters slant in the same direction.

Copy the following statement, or do one of your own! I love to practice writing in cursive. It makes me feel very grown-up!

Day 8

Get a dictionary and look up the following words and write the special spelling for each word in the blank provided. Put in all the markings.

EXAMPLE: magnolia <u>mag</u> <u>nōl'</u> <u>yə</u>. <u>Remember:</u> The special spelling tells you how to say a word correctly, how many syllables there are, where they are divided, and which syllable is stressed.

1. porcupine _____
2. electromagnet _____
3. elate _____
4. gravity _____
5. labor _____

6. cupboard _____
7. chisel _____
8. testify _____
9. nitrate _____
10. violinist _____

Choose three words from above and write their meaning.

1. word _____ meaning _____
2. word _____ meaning _____
3. word _____ meaning _____

We taste things because of our tongue and nose. The smell helps our tongue taste things. Ask your parents if you can taste some foods you have in your house. Tell whether they are bitter, sour, sweet, or salty. Write the name of the food you tasted under the correct heading.

EXAMPLE:

Bitter	Sour	Sweet	Salty
	lemon		

Complete the times table wheels.

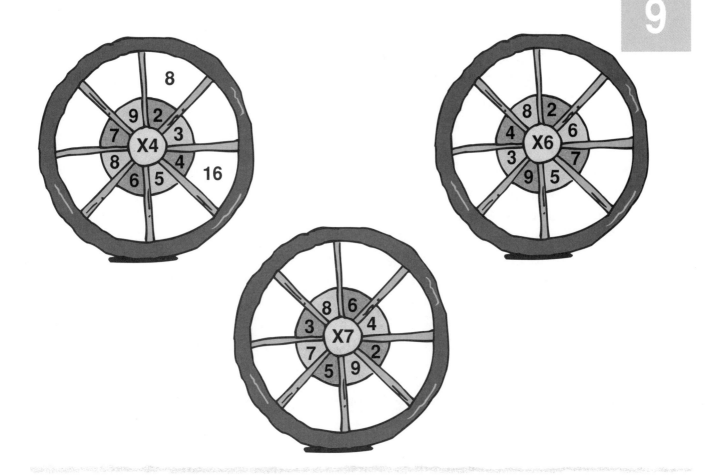

Underline the base, or root, word in each word.

blossoms	immediately	wreckage	incorrect
misspelled	inspector	retrace	reappear
exporting	invention	exhausted	messages

Underline the prefix in each word.

unusual	microphone	submarine	disappoint
displeased	invisible	extend	misplace
defrost	encircle	recover	enlarge

Underline the suffix in each word.

happiness	silently	tiniest	potatoes
hesitated	pleasantly	hasty	scarcely
mouthful	careless	graceful	spelling

Read each sentence. Put an F in the blank if the sentence is a fact. Write an O if it is an opinion. The first one has been done for you.

1. Christmas is always on the 25th of December. _____ _F_
2. Springtime is everyone's favorite time of year. _____
3. Birthdays are always a fun day for everyone. _____
4. Daylight and nighttime depend on the sun. _____
5. Dogs are said to be a man's best friend. _____
6. A spaceship travels faster than any airplane. _____
7. Lava rock was once a hot liquid. _____
8. Eating too much candy is hard on your teeth. _____
9. Most children like hot dogs and ice cream. _____
10. There are always twelve months in every year. _____
11. Diamonds are harder than cement. _____
12. Reading is one of the most important things in our lives. _____

Making Comparisons. Cut an apple in half, draw a picture of it, and label the parts. Draw a picture of the earth. Pretend that you cut a section out. Label its parts.

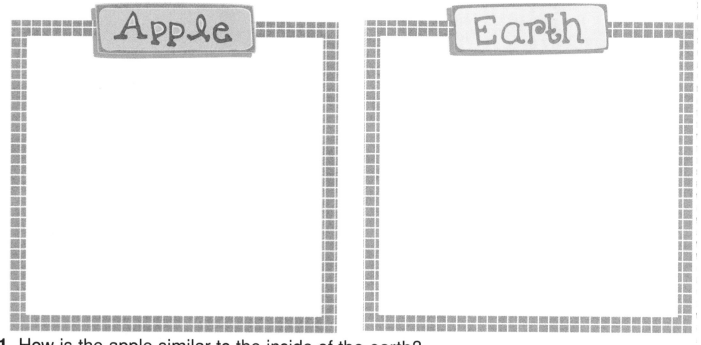

Apple

Earth

1. How is the apple similar to the inside of the earth?

_____

_____

2. How is the apple different from the inside of the earth?

_____

_____

Match the division and multiplication problems that are related.

EXAMPLE:

12 ÷ 4	5 x 5	38 ÷ 2	13 x 5
16 ÷ 8	3 x 4	63 ÷ 3	22 x 4
15 ÷ 5	9 x 4	50 ÷ 2	19 x 2
24 ÷ 6	6 x 4	84 ÷ 3	21 x 3
36 ÷ 9	9 x 5	56 ÷ 4	43 x 2
45 ÷ 5	3 x 5	86 ÷ 2	25 x 2
28 ÷ 7	7 x 4	88 ÷ 4	18 x 4
20 ÷ 4	2 x 8	65 ÷ 5	14 x 4
64 ÷ 8	5 x 4	80 ÷ 5	28 x 3
25 ÷ 5	8 x 8	72 ÷ 4	16 x 5
81 ÷ 9	8 x 9	51 ÷ 3	20 x 3
72 ÷ 9	8 x 6	86 ÷ 2	43 x 2
48 ÷ 6	9 x 9	72 ÷ 18	17 x 3
42 ÷ 7	6 x 7	60 ÷ 3	18 x 4

Look at the first word in each row. Circle the other words in the row that have the same vowel sound. Write a word of your own to go with the others with the same vowel sound.

1. team —	treat	chief	earth	sheep	_____
2. toast —	bowl	cow	both	though	_____
3. group —	truth	jump	cool	troop	_____
4. roll —	boat	stole	pool	told	_____
5. scoop —	droop	juice	soup	cook	_____
6. yawn —	jaws	chose	salt	lawn	_____
7. twice —	died	buy	since	price	_____
8. third —	church	torn	earth	fern	_____

Can you put the words in these mixed-up sentences in order to make sense?

1. flowers knows Jennifer to plant how

_____

_____

2. night could rainbows there at be

_____

_____

3. sky the into hot balloon up went air the

_____

_____

4. nobody new name knows the person's

_____

_____

Answer the questions about the underlined word in each sentence. Use a dictionary if you need one.

1. He is a <u>skillful</u> artist.
   a. What is the suffix in the word?   _____
   b. How would you divide the word into syllables?   _____
   c. What is the base word?   _____

2. A <u>harquebus</u> is an early type of firearm.
   a. How many syllables does the word have?   _____
   b. Is it a compound word?   _____
   c. What is the vowel sound in the last syllable?   _____

3. I was <u>heartbroken</u> when my puppy was run over by a car.
   a. What are the two words in this compound word?
      _____ and _____
   b. How many syllables does it have?   _____
   c. What is the base word for <u>broken</u>?   _____

4. You acted in a <u>disorderly</u> manner.
   a. What does this word mean?   _____
   b. Write it the special spelling way.   _____
   c. What is the prefix in this word?   _____
   d. What is the suffix?   _____

Estimate. Circle the answer you think is best.

1. A bathtub would hold (10 quarts or 10 gallons) of water.
2. A flower vase would hold (1 pint or 1 gallon) of water.
3. A fishbowl would hold (3 quarts or 3 cups) of water.
4. A big glass would hold (1 pint or 1 quart) of milk.
5. A bicycle would weigh (20 ounces or 20 pounds).
6. An orange would weigh (7 ounces or 7 pounds).
7. A new pencil would weigh (1 ounce or 1 pound).
8. A cob of corn would be (11 inches or 11 yards) long.
9. A new pencil would be (7 inches or 7 yards) long.
10. You could walk (1 yard or 1 mile) in ten minutes.
11. You could climb a high hill in (2 hours or 2 minutes).
12. A person could read a 1,500-page book in (16 minutes or 16 hours).

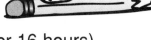

Negative words are words with <u>no</u> or <u>not</u> in them.
Don't use two <u>not</u>-words or <u>no</u>-words together.
Underline the correct answer.

> EXAMPLE: Don't be no litter bug. wrong
> Don't be a litter bug.   right

1. There aren't (no, any) letters for you today.
2. I don't (ever, never) get to go camping.
3. Most snakes don't hurt (anybody, nobody).
4. Rob bumped his head; he doesn't remember (nothing, anything).
5. I (haven't, have) never flown in a jet.
6. I don't have (no, any) work left to do.
7. There is never (anything, nothing) fun to do on Saturday.
8. Can't (nobody, anybody) fix this step?

Read this story and answer the questions by drawing your own conclusions.

Julie Ann and Clint closed their eyes to shut out the sun's glare. As they lay on the ground, the hot July sun felt good. They could hear the wind blowing ever so softly through the pine trees, making a kind of whispering, murmuring sound. They could hear the creek nearby making soothing, babbling sounds. They could even hear the distant screech of a hawk flying high in the sky overhead.

1. Where do you think they were?

_____

2. What season of the year is it?

_____

3. What other creatures do you think could be there?

_____

4. What would you like to do if you were there?

_____

Design a funny or clever birthday party invitation.

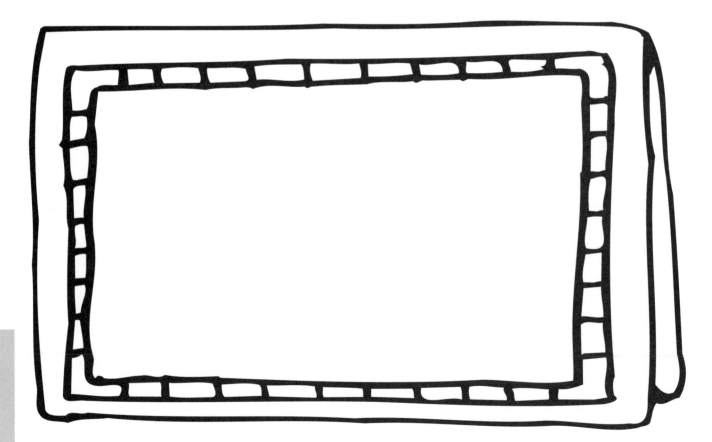

Find the sums.

246	500	924	402	550	465
+ 129	+ 806	+ 289	+ 629	+ 758	+ 398

1,284	7,762	3,383	4,290	4,006	5,642
+ 2,629	+ 1,473	+ 5,007	+ 2,968	+ 6,974	+ 9,280

9,542	2,423	3,252	6,666	1,920	9,040
+ 695	+ 1,932	+ 4,008	+ 4,208	+ 1,940	+ 1,070

An adjective is a word that describes a noun. Fill in the blanks with adjectives.

EXAMPLE: The bathroom is <u>red</u>. Deer have <u>sharp</u> antlers.

1. A _____ family moved in next door yesterday.

2. The bear has _____, _____ fur.

3. The _____ birds woke me up this morning.

4. Her _____, _____ balloon floated away.

5. Cotton and feathers are _____.

Some adjectives tell which ones. Use <u>this</u> and <u>that</u> with singular nouns, <u>these</u> and <u>those</u> with plural nouns.

1. _____ kittens are making too much noise.

2. _____ book is too long for me to read.

3. Is _____ one the hat Mom wanted?

4. _____ planet is very far away.

5. _____ ducks didn't come back to the pond this year.

Read the paragraph and answer the questions below.

Ann and her brother took swimming lessons this summer. Because they lived in the country, they had to take a bus to the pool. It took a half hour to get there. Their lessons were two hours long, and then they had to ride the bus home. Even though it took a lot of time, they enjoyed it very much, and by the end of the summer, they both knew how to swim well.

Circle the letter of the best summary for this paragraph.

a. Ann and her brother took swimming lessons this summer.

b. Ann and her brother rode a bus to the pool to take swimming lessons this summer. They enjoyed it and both learned how to swim.

Answer these questions.

1. Should a summary be longer or shorter than the original paragraph?

_____

2. What information should be in the summary?

_____

It is almost time for school to start. You are going shopping for new school clothes. Draw and color some of the clothes and things you would like for school this year.

Solve these problems.

1. Don was picking apples. He put 36 apples in each box. How many apples did he put in 9 boxes?

_____

2. Miss Brown has 25 children in her class. She wants to make 5 teams for a relay race. How many children will be on each team?

_____

3. Ted has $9.00 saved toward buying a new ball. He will get $3.00 today from his father. How much more will he need to buy the $19.95 ball?

4. Judy saved 867 pennies in May, 942 in July, and 716 in June. How many pennies did she save in these three months? _____ How many more pennies did she save in July than June?

_____

5. Lou needed 5 dozen eggs for a picnic. How many eggs does he need?

_____

6. Fred got a pie for his birthday. He ate 1/2 of the pie that day. He ate 1/4 of it the next day. How much did he have left?

_____

Use <u>the</u> before singular and plural nouns.
Use <u>a</u> or <u>an</u> before singular nouns only.
Use <u>a</u> before words beginning with consonant sounds.
Use <u>an</u> before words beginning with vowel sounds.

Fill in the blanks. Use <u>a</u>, <u>the</u>, <u>an</u>.

1. _____ orange rolled out of my sock.
2. That spider is _____ useful creature.
3. _____ ice fell off the roof.
4. Have you ever seen _____ octopus?
5. I love to watch _____ parrots when I go to _____ zoo.
6. My mother lost _____ earring.
7. My brother, Ron, can play _____ drum.
8. _____ floor is covered with newspapers.
9. _____ big, black bird ate the pie.
10. _____ alligator can be very dangerous.

Where would you find the answers to the following questions? Write the name of the reference aid you would use on the line.

| globe | dictionary | encyclopedia |

1. Where is Utah? _____
2. How do they harvest sugar cane in Hawaii? _____
3. Which syllable is stressed in the word <u>profit</u>? _____
4. What kind of food do people eat in Mexico? _____
5. Which continent is closest to Australia? _____
6. Where is the Indian Ocean? _____
7. Who was Thomas Edison, and what did he do? _____
8. What does <u>hibernate</u> mean? _____
9. Where do you find guide words? _____
10. Was England involved in the Second World War? _____
11. Is <u>knight</u> spelled correctly? _____
12. Where is the North Pole? _____

Choose the correct spelling for the following words. Fill in the circle.

EXAMPLE: ○ babys   ○ babeys   ● babies   ○ babby

1. ○ storys	○ stories	○ storyes	○ storiees
2. ○ crid	○ cryed	○ cried	○ kried
3. ○ seiling	○ ceiling	○ cieling	○ sieling
4. ○ certain	○ sertin	○ cirtaen	○ sertain
5. ○ citty	○ cite	○ sity	○ city
6. ○ matr	○ matter	○ mator	○ mater
7. ○ sound	○ soun	○ sownd	○ sounde
8. ○ ucross	○ acos	○ ecross	○ across
9. ○ pagge	○ pag	○ page	○ jage
10. ○ curcus	○ circus	○ sircus	○ circuse
11. ○ wouldn't	○ woodn't	○ woun't	○ wouldent
12. ○ singer	○ singir	○ singor	○ cinger
13. ○ hopefull	○ hoopfull	○ hopeful	○ hopful

Do these problems. Be sure to look at the signs. Use a calculator to help you if you have one.

25 - 5 = _____　　28 ÷ 4 = _____　　11 x 11 = _____

6 x 1 = _____　　14 ÷ 7 = _____　　36 - 16 = _____

36 ÷ 6 = _____　　16 + 6 = _____　　18 ÷ 3 = _____

5 x 6 = _____　　18 - 8 = _____　　9 x 2 = _____

17 + 3 = _____　　10 x 3 = _____　　7 x 7 = _____

11 + 8 = _____　　7 - 3 = _____　　81 ÷ 9 = _____

19 - 4 = _____　　22 - 2 = _____　　24 + 12 = _____

4 x 2 = _____　　7 x 6 = _____　　54 ÷ 9 = _____

9 ÷ 3 = _____　　3 x 7 = _____　　93 - 10 = _____

12 ÷ 3 = _____　　84 - 80 = _____　　6 x 8 = _____

4 + 4 = _____　　2 x 10 = _____　　9 + 6 = _____

10 ÷ 5 = _____　　12 - 6 = _____　　10 x 10 = _____

Here are some more spelling words. Practice writing them in cursive. Then have someone give you a test on them. Use another piece of paper.

EXAMPLE:

probably _probably_____

sincerely _____

minute _____

guest _____

similar _____

remember _____

smooth _____

garage _____

living _____

jeans _____

once _____

knobby _____

YOUR Test Score

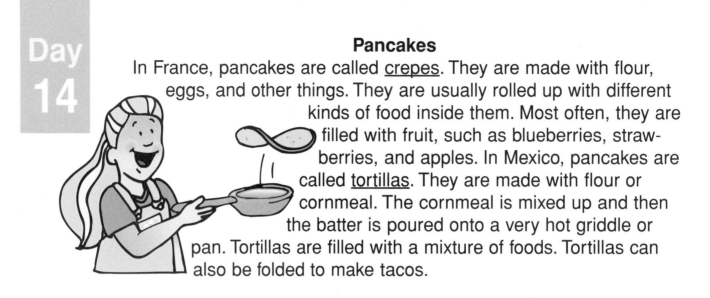

Pancakes

In France, pancakes are called <u>crepes</u>. They are made with flour, eggs, and other things. They are usually rolled up with different kinds of food inside them. Most often, they are filled with fruit, such as blueberries, strawberries, and apples. In Mexico, pancakes are called <u>tortillas</u>. They are made with flour or cornmeal. The cornmeal is mixed up and then the batter is poured onto a very hot griddle or pan. Tortillas are filled with a mixture of foods. Tortillas can also be folded to make tacos.

Write a recipe for your favorite pancakes and describe what you like to have on them.

_____

_____

_____

_____

We need the right kinds of food to keep us well and happy. Below are the major food groups. Name all the foods you can think of for each group. Write at least five for each.

<u>Meat and Protein</u>	<u>Fruit and Vegetables</u>	<u>Bread and Cereal</u>	<u>Milk and Dairy</u>

Subtract to find the differences.

| 5,042 | 2,710 | 4,200 | 7,106 | 3,340 | 9,824 |
| -1,624 | -1,624 | -1,122 | -2,410 | -1,112 | -1,224 |

| 6,831 | 7,605 | 6,351 | 8,001 | 4,232 | 1,898 |
| -4,560 | -1,282 | -5,675 | -2,381 | - 624 | - 197 |

| 2,356 | 9,010 | 3,542 | 5,600 | 7,575 | 4,230 |
| -2,147 | -2,167 | -1,004 | -2,983 | - 58 | -1,606 |

Commas in a series give meaning to the sentences. Choose the correct sentence.

1. Five children went on a bus to the zoo.

_____Jeannie, Julie Ann, John, Dennis, and Dave went together.

_____Jeannie, Julie, Ann, John, Dennis, and Dave went together.

2. There are three things to eat for lunch today.

_____We have chicken, sandwiches, carrot sticks, and soup.

_____We have chicken sandwiches, carrot sticks, and soup.

3. "I want to know where John is," Henry said.

_____"Where is John Henry?"

_____"Where is John, Henry?"

4. Ted can't find his four sisters.

_____Mary Ellen, Sue Tanya, Rachel, and Lisa are hiding.

_____Mary, Ellen, Sue, Tanya, Rachel, and Lisa are hiding.

Read the main idea sentence and the details below. Put an X before each detail important to the main idea.

One Saturday, Mike took his little sister, Judy, for a walk.

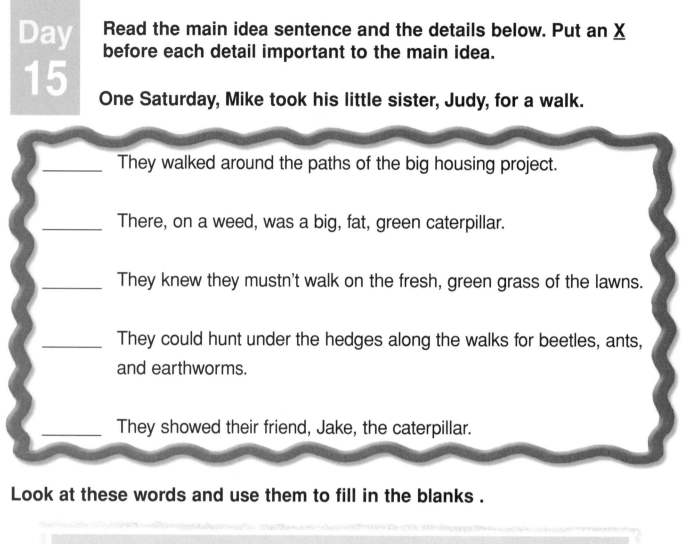

_____ They walked around the paths of the big housing project.

_____ There, on a weed, was a big, fat, green caterpillar.

_____ They knew they mustn't walk on the fresh, green grass of the lawns.

_____ They could hunt under the hedges along the walks for beetles, ants, and earthworms.

_____ They showed their friend, Jake, the caterpillar.

Look at these words and use them to fill in the blanks .

| enough | tube | brought | fantastic |
| where | woman | through | daughter |

1. Which word ends with the same sound as <u>lipstick</u>? _____

2. Which word rhymes with <u>ought</u>? _____

3. Which word begins the same as <u>what</u>? _____

4. Which word has the same vowel sound as <u>too</u>? _____

5. Write the spelling words that make a pair.
   son _____ man _____

6. Write the spelling word that ends with the same sound as <u>off</u>.
   _____

7. What word ends with the same sound as <u>chew</u>? _____

Words to Sound, Read, and Spell

heaving	invited	mane	necklaces	peacocks	powerful	remarked
height	island	manners	needles	peaked	practice	remember
helpful	jerked	maple	needless	peanut	practiced	repair
hibernate	jeweler	march	needn't	pedal	prairie	repeat
hibernation	jewelry	market	neighbors	peek	prancing	replied
hinges	jewels	marriage	nephew	peeped	prepare	report
hitched	joyful	married	nerves	peered	preparing	rescue
holiday	joyous	masterpiece	nibble	pencil	presents	resist
hollow	juice	match	niche	pendant	price	restaurant
holly	kennel	matter	nickel	penny	prickle	retire
homestretch	kettle	meadow	nightingales	pepper	prickly	returned
homework	key ring	meanwhile	noisy	pepperoni	princess	reward
hometown	kiln	measure	northern	perch	privilege	ribbon
honest	knapsack	measuring	notebook	perfect	probably	ridges
honey	kneading	medal	noticed	performance	problem	rise
honor	knees	melody	nuisance	person	project	risen
hooks	knelt	members	nurse	photographer	promise	rising
hopeful	known	mention	oatmeal	photographs	promised	roamed
hopped	lady's	mere	oats	piano	properly	roared
horrible	lamely	merrily	occasion	piccolo	protect	roast
horrified	language	message	odor	pickles	protected	rockets
horror	lash	metal	offered	picture	protesting	rodeo
horseback	laughter	mewing	offstage	pillow	proudly	route
hospital	leaden	midair	often	pinch	pump	royal
hotel	leadership	million	omelets	pinwheels	punished	ruin
hotter	leaned	minerals	onions	pitch	puppies	ruined
huddled	leap	minutes	opposite	pitcher	purest	saddle
hundred	leathery	mischief	orchard	pizza	puzzled	safety
hundredth	ledge	miserable	ordered	plains	quarreled	sagged
hungry	lies	missing	otherwise	plane	quarter	sailors
hurrah	liked	mistake	outdoors	playful	quills	salad
hurricane	likely	mistaken	owned	pleaded	quilt	salute
hushed	limbs	mists	paced	pleasant	quit	sandwich
hustle	lime	mixed-up	pacing	plenty	quite	sank
imagination	loaded	mixture	packages	plows	raccoons	sauce
imagine	lobster	moan	paddles	plug	raced	saucepan
imaginings	local	moaned	paid	plumped	radiator	scale
immediately	locked	modern	pain	plunge	ragged	scampered
important	lonesome	moment	palm	pocket	raise	scarlet
imprint	longer	monkey	pancakes	poems	raised	scattered
inaugural	longingly	moths	pantry	poet	rambling	scent
inched	loose	motion	paprika	pointed	rare	scientist
include	louder	motionless	parade	pokes	rather	scientists
inner	loudly	motorcycle	parakeet	poles	rattling	scissors
inning	loudspeaker	mule	pardon	police	realized	scold
insects	loved	munches	parkas	polished	real-life	scooped
instance	lovely	mural	parrot	politely	rear	scorched
instant	luckiest	murmured	parsley	ponies	reasons	scowled
instruments	lucky	museum	partly	porcupines	receive	scrambled
insurance	magical	mushroom	passengers	portrait	reckon	screamed
intercepted	magician	mushy	password	possessions	reddish	scribbled
interrupted	magnifying	mussel	patio	postcard	reins	scuffed
invented	mailbox	narrator	patriotic	posters	rejoiced	scuffling
inventors	major	narrow	patterns	pounced	relations	seamstress
invisible	mammals	native	paused	pound	relief	searched
invite	managed	naughty	peaches	pouting	remarkable	

Words to Sound, Read, and Spell

seated	slim	sprawling	supper	tiniest	unless	whom
seeped	slimy	sprinkle	supply	title	unpack	whooping
seized	slingshot	square	support	toast	unreasonable	wiggle
selfish	slipped	squashing	suppose	toenails	unspoken	wiggly
sentence	slippery	squirrel	supposed	tomato	untied	willow
serious	slunk	stables	surrounds	tough	untouched	wilted
servants	small	stack	sustaining	tour	unusual	winced
served	smaller	stairs	swallow	toured	unwrapped	window
setting	smallish	stalls	swamp	tourists	upward	windowpane
seventy	smile	stamp	sweaters	toward	urged	windy
several	smiled	starfish	sweep	towel	urgent	winked
sewing	smiling	starless	swell	towers	useless	wizard
shadow	smock	started	swept	townspeople	usually	women
shafts	smoky	starved	swiftly	trace	valve	wondered
shaggy	smudges	station	swing	traffic	vegetable	wonderful
shame	snails	steady	swinging	travel	view	wonderfully
sharp	snarl	steepest	swirled	traveled	vines	won't
sharpest	sneakers	steer	swirling	treasure	violet	woodchucks
shave	sneaking	sternly	swollen	trembled	volunteer	wooden
sheet	sneezed	sting	swooped	trombone	wade	wore
shelter	snowplow	stockings	swung	trooped	wagged	workbench
shimmering	snug	stony	syrup	trotted	wagon	world
shining	snuggled	stoop	system	trouble	wander	worn
shocking	soaked	store-bought	tablespoons	trough	wandered	worse
shop	soar	stork	tackle	trudged	warmth	worst
short	soften	storyteller	tame	truly	warned	worthless
shoulders	solid	stoutness	tandem	trumpet	warns	worthy
shouldn't	solution	straight	tangled	trusts	wasn't	wouldn't
shovel	somebody	strain	tasted	truth	waste	wound
shrieked	someday	strained	taught	tuba	wasted	wounds
shrugged	somehow	strapped	teasing	tuff	watch	wrinkled
sickness	someone	strength	television	tugboats	watchful	wrists
sideways	somersaults	stretched	tender	tumbling	weak	written
sifted	sort	strike	tent	tummy	weakly	yeast
signal	sour	stringer	tenth	tundra	wealthiest	yellowish
silence	south	strip	terrible	tuneful	weight	yelping
silent	southwest	strips	terribly	tunnel	welcome	yesterday
silver	spaceship	stroked	test	turquoise	wept	you'll
silversmith	sparkled	strokes	tested	twenty	we're	you're
similar	sped	stubborn	thankful	twice	weren't	yourself
simple	speeches	students	they'll	twigs	we've	yourselves
since	spell	studied	they're	twilight	whack	yummy
singer	spend	studio	they've	twinkle	whales	zebra
single	spent	stunned	third	twists	wheat	zigzagging
sinkers	spicy	stylish	though	unable	wheelbarrow	zwieback
sizzle	spill	subject	thought	unbuttoning	wheelchair	
skeletons	spilled	succeeded	thoughtfully	uncle	wheezed	
skidding	spite	success	thousands	uncomfortable	whenever	
skipper	splat	successful	thrashing	uncommon	whether	
slab	splatters	sudden	throat	underground	whipped	
slenderer	splendid	suddenly	through	understands	whirl	
slept	splints	suggested	thrown	undressing	whiskers	
slice	splash	sunrise	thrust	uneasily	whisper	
slicing	sports	sunset	tide	unfamiliar	whistle	
slide	sprained	super	tightly	unhappy	whitened	
slightly	sprang	supermarkets	tightness	uniforms	whole	

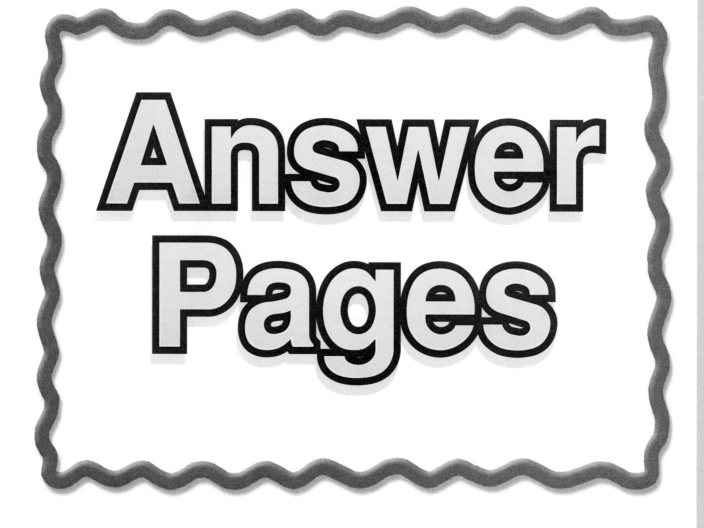

Answer Pages

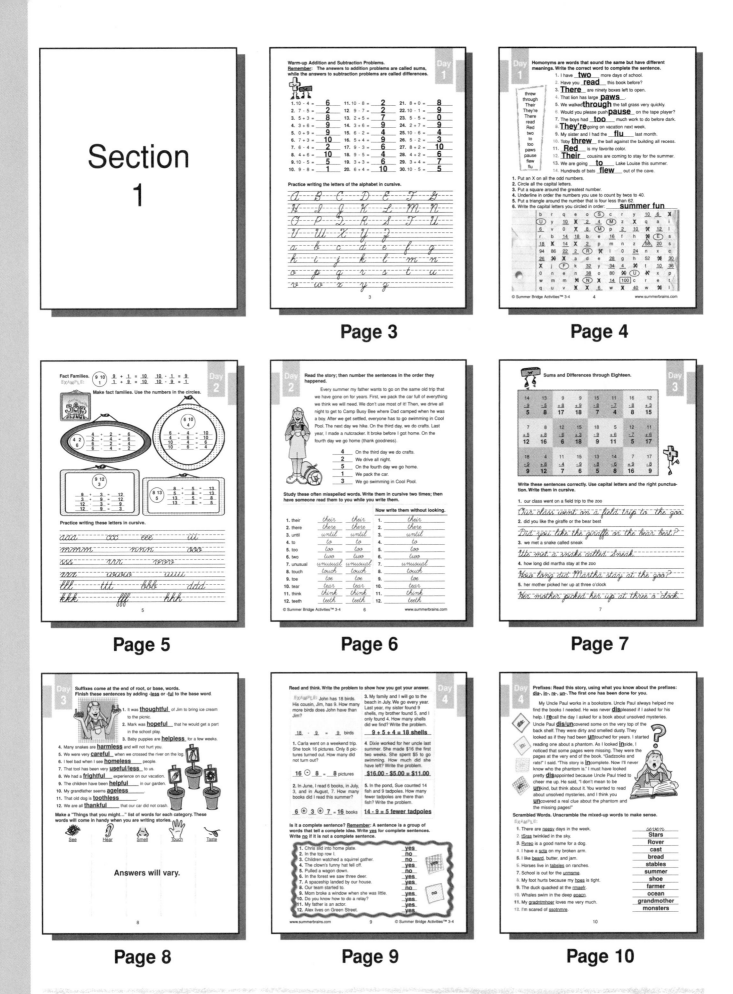

Section 1

Page 3

Page 4

Page 5

Page 6

Page 7

Page 8

Page 9

Page 10

Page 11

Day 5

Place Value. Write the numbers.

6 tens	9 ones	5 tens	10 tens
8 ones	4 tens	0 ones	0 ones
68	**49**	**50**	**100**

6 tens	4 hundreds	5 ones	9 hundreds
3 hundreds	0 tens	6 hundreds	3 ones
8 ones	2 ones	7 tens	5 tens
368	**402**	**675**	**953**

Write these numbers.

8. five hundred sixty-one **561**
9. four hundred eighty-six **486**
10. two hundred ninety-nine **299**
11. eight hundred **800**
12. one hundred fifty **150**
13. seven hundred thirty-two **732**

How many gumballs in each set?

Ex. **221**
14. **411**
15. **213**
16. **330**
17. **132**

Divide these compound words into three categories. Write in cursive.

skyline, grapevine, raindrop, hindsight, drumstick, handbag, bluebell, landscape, oatmeal, suitcase, wishbone, hitchhike, goldfinch, themselves, limestone, showboat, thumbtack

1. long vowel combinations
skyline, grapevine, hindsight, oatmeal, suitcase, limestone, showboat.

2. short vowel combinations
drumstick, handbag, themselves, thumbtack

3. long and short vowel combinations
raindrop, bluebell, landscape, wishbone, hitchhike, goldfinch

11

Page 12

Day 5

Word Meanings. Write a word for each meaning.

| knead | sense | praise | dull | guide | amazing |
| wheat | coast | numb | certain | towel | purchase |

1. not able to feel — **numb**
2. we do this to dough — **knead**
3. to be sure — **certain**
4. to buy something — **purchase**
5. to see, hear, feel, taste, smell — **sense**
6. flour is made from — **wheat**
7. a leader of a group — **guide**
8. to say something nice — **praise**
9. something wonderful can be — **amazing**
10. a knife that is not sharp — **dull**
11. where the ocean and the land meet — **coast**
12. used to dry yourself — **towel**

Write the sentences that are true.

1. We are camping in the forest.
2. The wind is blowing the clouds at night.
3. It is raining.
4. We are fishing.
5. We are safe inside.

1. We are camping in the forest.
3. It is raining.
5. We are safe inside.

12

Page 13

Day 6

How many ways can you make the amount of money shown in these problems? Use real money to help you.

Ex. **10¢**
10 pennies
2 nickels
1 nickel, 5 pennies
1 dime

3. **$1.00**

1. **25¢**

4. **$1.60**

Answers will vary.

2. **50¢**

5. **$2.40**

Circle the nouns. Underline the verbs. Remember: Nouns name things and verbs show action.

elephant, sang, ate, fixed, laugh, beg, tent, Mr. Chip, team, book, California, guitar, landed, Lake Street, freight, cleaned, yell, plays, fly, visited, Kent, write, run, strength, swim, engine, jump, broccoli, leap, letters, June, shakes, Marsha, dentist, friend, walk

13

Page 14

Day 6

Use the word bank to make compound words answering the descriptions.

EXAMPLE:

Word Bank

bath	apple
space	storm
team	ship
horse	tub
snow	back
scare	side
post	card
hill	brows
eye	mates
pine	crow

1. A place your mom sends you to get clean. **bathtub**
2. A fruit that is good to eat. **pineapple**
3. What farmers put in cornfields to scare birds away. **scarecrow**
4. A kind of weather some people get in the wintertime. **snowstorm**
5. If you're on a horse, you have this kind of ride. **horseback**
6. A place that might be grassy, high up, and a good place for a picnic. **hillside**
7. A type of mail you can write and send to a friend. **postcard**
8. People who play sports with you. **teammates**
9. What you should find on your face above your eyelashes. **eyebrows**
10. What astronauts might fly in. **spaceship**

You are lost in the forest for a long time with nothing but a knife, a few matches, and one pan. How and where will you live? What will you do? What will you eat?

Stories will vary.

14

Page 15

Day 7

Rounding Numbers. Round to the nearest ten.

EXAMPLE:
28 = 20 or 30, because 28 is nearer to 30 than to 20.
65 = 60 or 70, because when a number is halfway, round it up to the larger number.
12 = 10 or 20, because 12 is nearer to 10 than it is to 20.

0 10 20 30 40 50 60 70

Circle the answer.

1. 63 = **60** or 70
2. 19 = 10 or **20**
3. 55 = 50 or **60**
4. 83 = **80** or 90
5. 27 = 20 or **30**

6. 99 = 90 or **100**
7. 25 = 20 or **30**
8. 12 = **10** or 20
9. 44 = **40** or 50
10. 36 = 30 or **40**

Ex. 28 = **30**
11. 44 = **40**
12. 13 = **10**
13. 85 = **90**
14. 33 = **30**

21 = **20**
15. 92 = **90**
16. 78 = **80**
17. 18 = **20**
18. 55 = **60**

Round to the nearest 100.

Ex. 297 = **300**
19. 211 = **200** or 300
20. 767 = 700 or **800**
21. 425 = **400** or 500

22. 841 = **800**
23. 587 = **600**
24. 699 = **700**

Rewrite this paragraph. Add the correct punctuation and capitalization.

last summer we went camping in colorado we went hiking and swimming every day one time i actually saw a little deer with spots and a white tail we also collected a lot of pretty rocks flowers and leaves we had a great time i didn't want to leave

Last summer we went camping in Colorado. We went hiking and swimming everyday. One time I actually saw a little deer with spots and a white tail. We also collected a lot of pretty rocks, flowers, and leaves. We had a great time! I didn't want to leave.

15

Page 16

Day 7

Circle the word that is divided into syllables correctly.

EXAMPLE: fif/teen **fift/een** fift/een fifte/en

1. cact/us	ca/ctus	**cac/tus**	c/actus
2. bli/ster	blist/er	**blis/ter**	bli/ister
3. **al/ways**	a/lways	alw/ays	alwa/ys
4. har/bor	ha/rbor	**harb/or**	harbo/r
5. fl/ower	flo/wer	flowe/r	**flow/er**
6. **bas/ket**	bask/et	ba/sket	baske/t
7. e/nclose	**en/close**	encl/ose	enclo/se
8. obe/ys	**o/beys**	ob/eys	obey/s
9. qu/estion	ques/tion	que/stion	**ques/tion**
10. sal/ute	salut/e	**sa/lute**	salu/te

Write the abbreviation for the following words. Be sure to put a period (.) at the end of each abbreviation.

EXAMPLE:

1. January — **Jan.**
2. February — **Feb.**
3. March — **Mar.**
4. April — **Apr.**
5. August — **Aug.**
6. October — **Oct.**
7. November — **Nov.**
8. December — **Dec.**
9. Sunday — **Sun.**
10. Monday — **Mon.**
11. Tuesday — **Tues.**
12. Wednesday — **Wed.**
13. Thursday — **Thur.**
14. Saturday — **Sat.**
15. Doctor — **Dr.**
16. Mister — **Mr.**
17. Mississippi — **Miss.**
18. Television — **T.V.**

16

Page 17

Day 8

Be sure to look at the ones, tens, hundreds, and thousands as you do the following problems.

Which number is greater? Circle your answer.

1. 126 / **261**
2. **342** / 231
3. 3,619 / **719**
4. **1,426** / 1,326
5. 2,510 / **3,510**
6. 1,629 / **1,639**

Write greater than (>) or less than (<) on the line.

Ex. 521 **<** than 121.
13. 371 is **<** than 367
14. 126 is **<** than 226
15. 808 is **>** than 801
16. 429 is **>** than 249
17. 762 is **>** than 761
18. 1,638 is **>** than 738
19. 4,206 is **<** than 5,206
20. 3,929 is **>** than 3,729
21. 5,340 is **<** than 5,940
22. 1,500 is **>** than 1,005

Circle the number that is less.

7. 580 / **579**
8. 999 / **899**
9. 624 / **524**
10. **1,200** / 1,201
11. **7,824** / 7,842
12. **5,555** / 5,846

Read the following words. Write the vowel you hear and mark if it's long or short.

EXAMPLE: fly ĭ **long**
went ĕ **short**

1. tie **i long**
2. puzzle **u short**
3. head **e short**
4. niece **e long**
5. bugle **u long**
6. plan **a short**
7. trail **a long**
8. chief **e long**
9. mule **u long**
10. toad **o long**
11. neck **e short**
12. high **i long**
13. sweat **e short**
14. bump **u short**
15. knot **o short**
16. ripped **i short**
17. find **i long**
18. chip **i short**
19. colt **o long**
20. sweep **e long**
21. patch **a short**
22. feather **e short**
23. juice **u long**
24. gray **a long**

www.summerbrains.com 17 © www.summerbrains.com

Page 18

Day 8

Use commas, add small words, or leave words out to combine the sentences.

EXAMPLE:
1. My friends' names are Wanda and Pete. I also like Mandy and Joe.
I like my friends Wanda, Pete, Mandy, and Joe.

2. Rats will chew on wood and bones. They will also chew on nuts and twigs.
Rats chew on wood, bones, nuts, and twigs.

3. Dogs and cats can be pets. Gerbils and hamsters can be pets, too.
Dogs, cats, gerbils, and hamsters can be pets.

4. I am wearing blue jeans and a striped shirt. My shoes are black, and my socks are green. On my head is a baseball cap.
I am wearing blue jeans, a stripped shirt, black shoes, green socks, and a baseball cap.

5. My teammates like ice cream, pie, and cake. They also like pizza, hamburgers, and hot dogs.
My teammates like ice cream, pie, cake, pizza, hamburgers, and hot dogs.

Read and follow directions. Read them through completely first. If you follow the directions carefully, you will find the name of an animal.

P L A E N H T E

1. Remove the letters L and the second E.
2. Put the LE at the beginning of the word.
3. Move the second E so it is at the beginning of the word.
4. Put an S at the end of the word.
5. Move the H so that it is between the P and the A.
6. Don't do step 4.
7. Write the name of the animal here.
ELEPHANT

18

Page 19

Day 9

More Than Thousands.

We read:

| 6,000 — six thousand |
| 60,000 — sixty thousand |
| 600,000 — six hundred thousand |

Read the following numbers aloud to a parent or an adult.

EXAMPLE:
50,231—fifty thousand two hundred thirty-one
765,326—seven hundred sixty-five thousand three hundred twenty-six

1. 92,126
2. 9,800
3. 87,124
4. 3,823
5. 40,000
6. 700,820
7. 328,984
8. 6,401
9. 10,822
10. 126,238
11. 7,069
12. 942,681
13. 31,010
14. 575,618
15. 202,435
16. 138,000
17. 16,126
18. 800,290
19. 1,999
20. 999,999

Make real words by writing ar, ir, or, er, ur, in the blanks.

h**or**se, n**ur**se, th**ir**ty, p**or**ch
h**ar**d, ch**ir**p, s**er**ve, b**ir**ch
g**ir**l, th**ir**st, t**ur**key, h**er**
ch**ar**ge, c**ur**b, m**ar**ch, y**ar**n
st**ar**t, sp**ar**k, sk**ir**t
c**ir**cus, c**or**n, rep**or**t, st**ar**ch
th**ir**sty, wh**ir**l, al**ar**m, t**ur**n
p**ur**se, g**er**m, c**ur**l, f**ir**st
b**ur**st, f**ar**m, v**er**b, ch**ur**ch

19

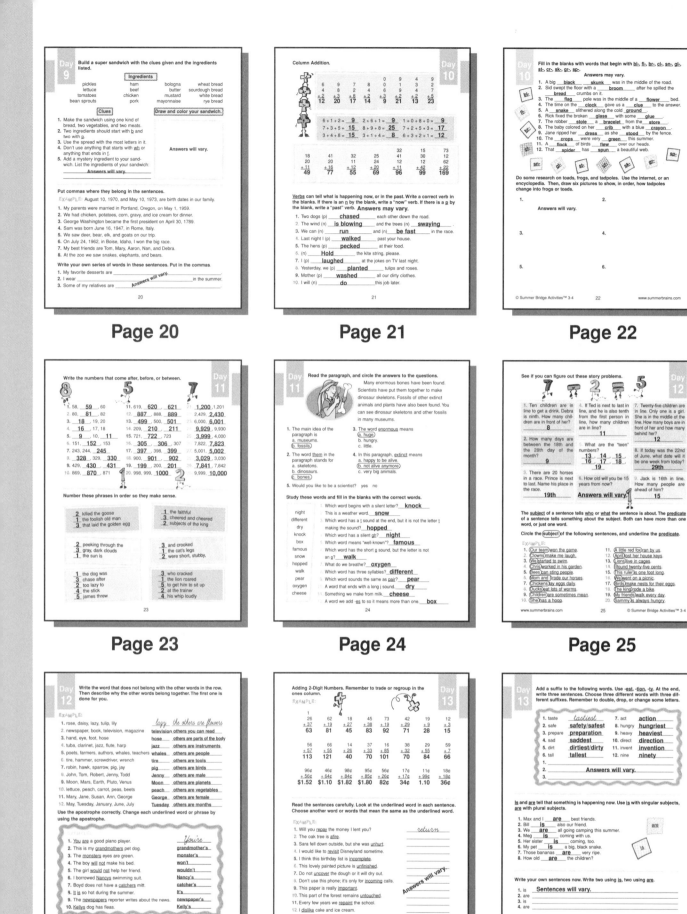

Page 20

Page 21

Page 22

Page 23

Page 24

Page 25

Page 26

Page 27

Page 28

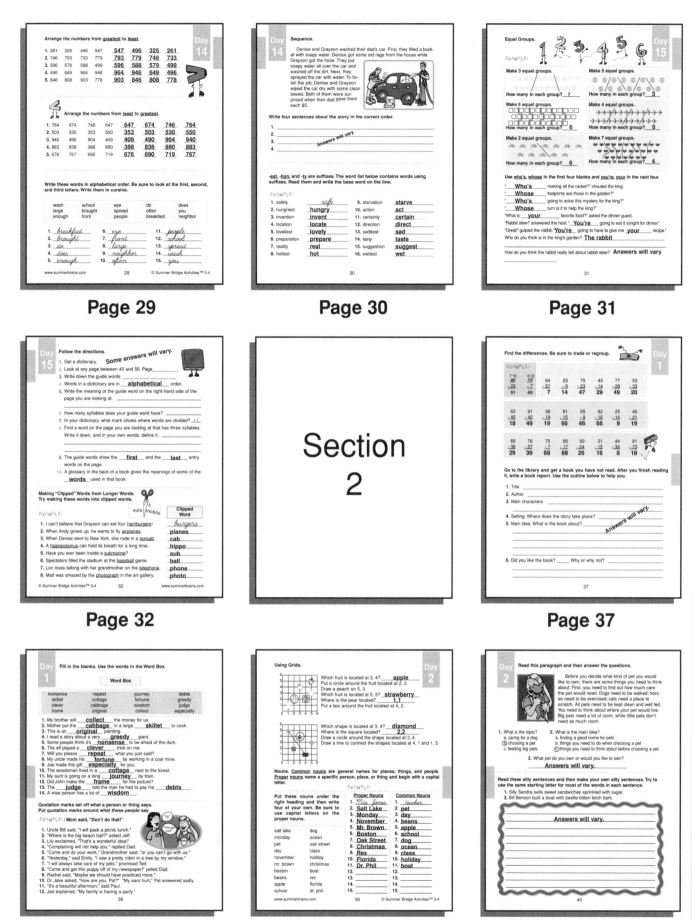

Page 29

Page 30

Page 31

Page 32

Section 2

Page 37

Page 38

Page 39

Page 40

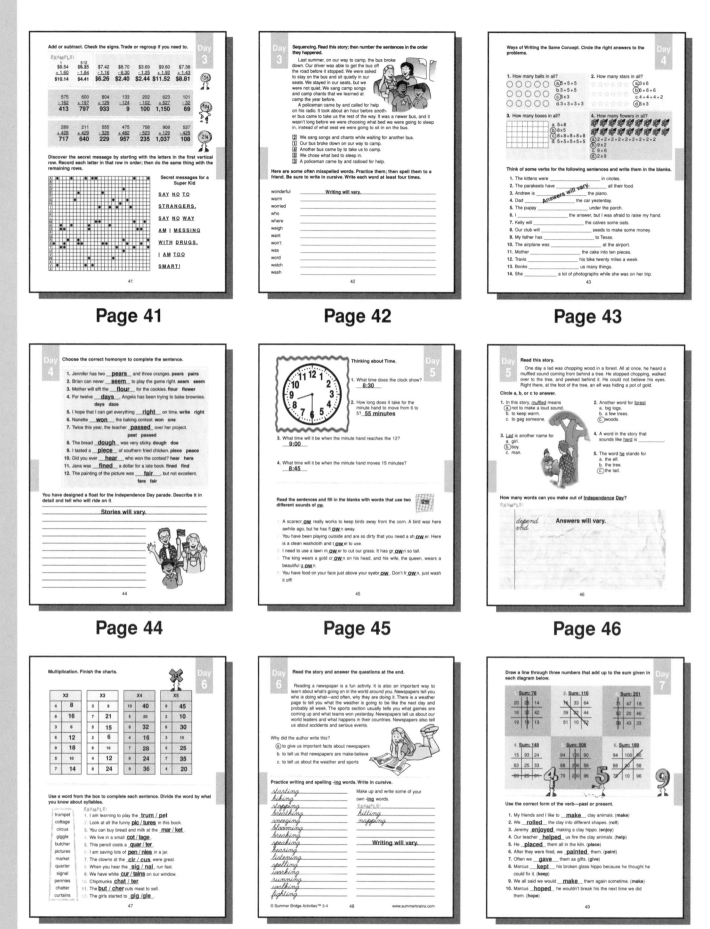

Page 41

Page 42

Page 43

Page 44

Page 45

Page 46

Page 47

Page 48

Page 49

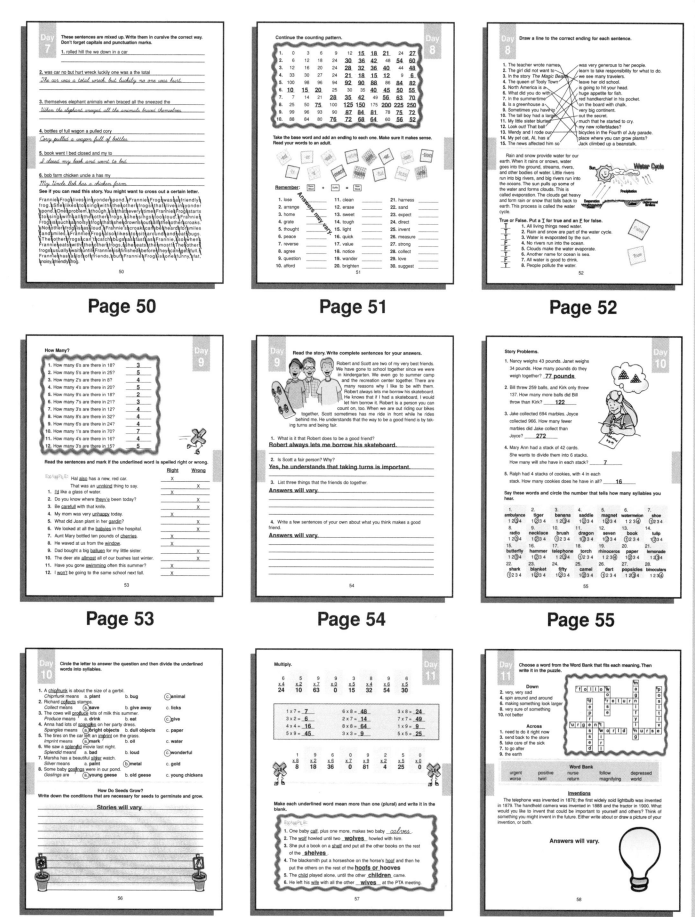

Page 50

Day 7 — These sentences are mixed up. Write them in cursive the correct way. Don't forget capitals and punctuation marks.

1. rolled hill the we down in a car

2. was car no but hurt wreck luckily one was a the total
The car was a total wreck, but luckily no one was hurt.

3. themselves elephant animals when braced all the sneezed the
When the elephant sneezed, all the animals braced themselves.

4. bottles of full wagon a pulled cory
Cory pulled a wagon full of bottles.

5. book went I bed closed and my to
I closed my book and went to bed.

6. bob farm chicken uncle a has my
My Uncle Bob has a chicken farm.

See if you can read this story. You might want to cross out a certain letter.

50

Page 51

Day 8 — Continue the counting pattern.

1.	0	3	6	9	**12**	**15**	**18**	**21**	24	**27**
2.	6	12	18	24	**30**	**36**	**42**	48	**54**	**60**
3.	12	16	20	24	**28**	**32**	**36**	**40**	44	**48**
4.	33	30	27	24	**21**	**18**	**15**	**12**	9	**6**
5.	100	98	96	94	**92**	**90**	**88**	86	**84**	**82**
6.	**10**	**15**	**20**	25	30	35	40	45	**50**	**55**
7.	7	14	21	**28**	**35**	**42**	49	**56**	**63**	**70**
8.	50	50	75	100	**125**	**150**	175	**200**	**225**	**250**
9.	99	96	93	90	**87**	**84**	**81**	78	**75**	**72**
10.	88	84	80	**76**	**72**	**68**	64	60	**56**	**52**

Take the base word and add an ending to each one. Make sure it makes sense. Read your words to an adult.

Remember: Base Word + Suffix = New Word

1. lose	11. clean	21. harness
2. arrange	12. erase	22. sand
3. home	13. sweet	23. expect
4. grate	14. tough	24. direct
5. thought	15. light	25. invent
6. peace	16. quick	26. measure
7. reverse	17. value	27. strong
8. agree	18. notice	28. collect
9. question	19. wander	29. love
10. afford	20. brighten	30. suggest

Answers may vary.

51

Page 52

Day 8 — Draw a line to the correct ending for each sentence.

1. The teacher wrote names
2. The girl did not want to
3. In the story *The Magic Beans*
4. The queen of Tooly Town
5. North America is a
6. What did you do with
7. In the summertime
8. Is a greenhouse a
9. Sometimes you have to
10. The tall boy had a large
11. My little sister blurted
12. Look out! That ball
13. Wendy and I rode our
14. My pet cat, Al, has a
15. The news affected him so

was very generous to her people.
learn to take responsibility for what to do.
we see many travelers.
leave her old school.
is going to hit your head.
huge appetite for fish.
red handkerchief in his pocket.
on the board with chalk.
very big continent.
out the secret.
much that he started to cry.
my new rollerblades?
bicycles in the Fourth of July parade.
place where you can grow plants?
Jack climbed up a beanstalk.

Rain and snow provide water for our earth. When it rains or snows, water goes into the ground, streams, rivers, and other bodies of water. Little rivers run into big rivers, and big rivers run into the oceans. The sun pulls up some of the water and forms clouds. The clouds get heavy and form rain or snow that falls back to earth. This process is called the water cycle.

True or False. Put a T for true and an F for false.

T 1. All living things need water.
T 2. Rain and snow are part of the water cycle.
T 3. Water is evaporated by the sun.
F 4. No rivers run into the ocean.
T 5. Clouds make the water evaporate.
F 6. Another name for ocean is sea.
F 7. All water is good to drink.
T 8. People pollute the water.

52

Page 53

How Many?

1. How many 6's are there in 18? **3**
2. How many 5's are there in 25? **5**
3. How many 2's are there in 8? **4**
4. How many 4's are there in 20? **5**
5. How many 9's are there in 18? **2**
6. How many 7's are there in 21? **3**
7. How many 3's are there in 12? **4**
8. How many 8's are there in 32? **4**
9. How many 6's are there in 24? **4**
10. How many 1's are there in 70? **70**
11. How many 4's are there in 16? **4**
12. How many 3's are there in 15? **5**

Day 9

Read the sentences and mark if the underlined word is spelled right or wrong.

	Right	Wrong
EXAMPLE: Hal <u>also</u> has a new, red car.	X	
That was an <u>unkind</u> thing to say.		X
1. I'd like a glass of water.	X	
2. Do you know where <u>they've</u> been today?		X
3. Be <u>carefull</u> with that knife.		X
4. My mom was very <u>unhappy</u> today.	X	
5. What did Joan plant in her <u>gardin</u>?		X
6. We looked at all the <u>babyies</u> in the hospital.		X
7. Aunt Mary bottled ten pounds of <u>cherries</u>.	X	
8. He waved at us from the <u>window</u>.	X	
9. Dad bought a big <u>balluen</u> for my little sister.		X
10. The deer ate <u>allmost</u> all of our bushes last winter.		X
11. Have you gone <u>swiming</u> often this summer?		X
12. I <u>won't</u> be going to the same school next fall.	X	

53

Page 54

Day 9 — Read the story. Write complete sentences for your answers.

Robert and Scott are two of my very best friends. We have gone to school together since we were in kindergarten. We even go to summer camp and the recreation center together. There are many reasons why I like to be with them. Robert always lets me borrow his skateboard. He knows that if I had a skateboard, I would let him borrow it. Robert is a person you can count on, too. When we are out riding our bikes together, Scott sometimes has me ride in front while he rides behind me. He understands that the way to be a good friend is by taking turns and being fair.

1. What is it that Robert does to be a good friend?
Robert always lets me borrow his skateboard.

2. Is Scott a fair person? Why?
Yes, he understands that taking turns is important.

3. List three things that the friends do together.
Answers will vary.

4. Write a few sentences of your own about what you think makes a good friend.
Answers will vary.

54

Page 55

Story Problems.

Day 10

1. Nancy weighs 43 pounds. Janet weighs 34 pounds. How many pounds do they weigh together? **77 pounds**

2. Bill threw 259 balls, and Kirk only threw 137. How many more balls did Bill throw than Kirk? **122**

3. Jake collected 694 marbles. Joyce collected 966. How many fewer marbles did Jake collect than Joyce? **272**

4. Mary Ann had a stack of 42 cards. She wants to divide them into 6 stacks. How many will she have in each stack? **7**

5. Ralph had 4 stacks of cookies, with 4 in each stack. How many cookies does he have in all? **16**

Say these words and circle the number that tells how many syllables you hear.

1. ambulance	2. tiger	3. banana	4. saddle	5. magnet	6. watermelon	7. shoe
1 2 ③ 4	1 ② 3 4	1 2 ③ 4	1 ② 3 4	1 ② 3 4	1 2 3 ④	① 2 3 4
8. radio	9. necklace	10. brush	11. dragon	12. seven	13. book	14. tulip
1 2 ③ 4	1 ② 3 4	① 2 3 4	1 ② 3 4	1 ② 3 4	① 2 3 4	1 ② 3 4
15. butterfly	16. hammer	17. telephone	18. torch	19. rhinoceros	20. paper	21. lemonade
1 2 ③ 4	1 ② 3 4	1 2 ③ 4	① 2 3 4	1 2 3 ④	1 ② 3 4	1 2 ③ 4
22. shark	23. blanket	24. fifty	25. camel	26. dart	27. popsicles	28. binoculars
① 2 3 4	1 ② 3 4	1 ② 3 4	1 ② 3 4	① 2 3 4	1 2 ③ 4	1 2 3 ④

55

Page 56

Day 10 — Circle the letter to answer the question and then divide the underlined words into syllables.

1. A <u>chipmunk</u> is about the size of a gerbil.
Chip/munk means a. plant b. bug c. **animal**
2. Richard <u>collects</u> stamps.
Col/lect means a. **save** b. give away c. licks
3. The cows will <u>produce</u> lots of milk this summer.
Pro/duce means a. drink b. eat c. **give**
4. Anna had lots of <u>spangles</u> on her party dress.
Span/gles means a. **bright objects** b. dull objects c. paper
5. The tires on the car left an <u>imprint</u> on the grass.
Im/print means a. **mark** b. oil c. water
6. We saw a <u>splendid</u> movie last night.
Splen/did means a. bad b. loud c. **wonderful**
7. Marsha has a beautiful <u>silver</u> watch.
Sil/ver means a. paint b. **metal** c. gold
8. Some baby <u>goslings</u> were in our pond.
Gos/lings are a. **young geese** b. old geese c. young chickens

How Do Seeds Grow?
Write down the conditions that are necessary for seeds to germinate and grow.

Stories will vary.

56

Page 57

Day 11 — Multiply.

6	5	9	9	3	8	9	6
x 4	x 2	x 7	x 0	x 5	x 4	x 6	x 5
24	10	63	0	15	32	54	30

1 x 7 = **7**	6 x 8 = **48**	3 x 8 = **24**
3 x 2 = **6**	2 x 7 = **14**	7 x 7 = **49**
4 x 4 = **16**	8 x 8 = **64**	1 x 9 = **9**
5 x 9 = **45**	3 x 3 = **9**	5 x 5 = **25**

1	9	6	0	9	2	5	0
x 8	x 2	x 6	x 7	x 9	x 2	x 5	x 0
8	18	36	0	81	4	25	0

Make each underlined word mean more than one (plural) and write it in the blank.

EXAMPLE:
1. One baby <u>calf</u>, plus one more, makes two baby **calves**.
2. The <u>wolf</u> howled until two **wolves** howled with him.
3. She put a book on a <u>shelf</u> and put all the other books on the rest of the **shelves**.
4. The blacksmith put a horseshoe on the horse's <u>hoof</u> and then he put the others on the rest of the **hoofs or hooves**.
5. The <u>child</u> played alone, until the other **children** came.
6. He left his <u>wife</u> with all the other **wives** at the PTA meeting.

57

Page 58

Day 11 — Choose a word from the Word Bank that fits each meaning. Then write it in the puzzle.

Down
2. very, very sad
4. spin around and around
6. making something look larger
8. very sure of something
10. not better

Across
1. need to do it right now
3. send back to the store
5. take care of the sick
7. to go after
9. the earth

Word Bank

urgent	positive	nurse	follow	depressed
worse	twirl	return	magnifying	world

Inventions

The telephone was invented in 1876; the first widely sold lightbulb was invented in 1879. The handheld camera was invented in 1888 and the tractor in 1900. What would you like to invent that could be important to yourself and others? Think of something you might invent in the future. Either write about or draw a picture of your invention, or both.

Answers will vary.

58

Page 59

Use the graph to answer the questions.

Ms. Fran has many friends. She sends them letters each week. Mark the answers to the questions on the graph. (Monday is done for you.) Each letter shown stands for four letters.

Mon. 🔲🔲
Tues. 🔲🔲🔲🔲
Wed. 🔲🔲🔲🔲🔲
Thurs. 🔲🔲🔲🔲
Fri. 🔲🔲🔲🔲🔲

1. How many letters did Ms. Fran send out on Thursday? **20**
2. On what two days did she send out the number? **Tues.** and **Fri.**
3. What was the fewest she sent in one day? **12**
4. What was the most that she sent in one day? **28**
5. How many letters did she send out altogether? **92**

Similarities and Differences. Look at each pair of words. Write down at least one way they are alike and at least one way they are different.

1. leopard and cheetah **Answers will vary.**

2. typewriter and piano

3. cabin and tent

4. whistle and sing

59

Page 60

Real or Make-Believe. Write M for make-believe and R for real.

R 1. A pumpkin growing on a vine in a field.
R 2. A fireman saving a kitten from a tree.
M 3. An elephant that can fly in a circus.
M 4. A cow that can give chocolate milk.
R 5. A family taking a summer vacation.
M 6. A chicken that lays golden eggs.
R 7. A brother and sister working together.
R 8. Five children going to a movie in the afternoon.
M 9. Buckets of paint turning the sky many colors.
M 10. A ghost turning a frog into a king.
R 11. A tree being blown over by the wind.
M 12. A rainbow bridge to the moon.
R 13. Going for a boat ride down the Mississippi.
M 14. A big tree growing overnight.
M 15. A giant who eats children.
M 16. A man who is seven-and-a-half feet tall.

Use the clue to help you fill in the missing letters. Hint: Use vowels.

1. to do something many times — O**f**ten
2. a sea animal with eight legs — **O**ct**o**pus
3. a reptile that lives in a swamp — cr**o**c**o**d**i**le
4. a very small house — c**o**tt**a**ge
5. something to keep the rain off — **u**mbr**e**lla
6. twelve things — d**o**z**e**n
7. a tree or the inner part of your hand — p**a**lm
8. two things that are different — **o**pp**o**s**i**te
9. a place that has little rain — de**s**e**r**t
10. you can put this on a Christmas tree — **o**rn**a**m**e**nt
11. a dessert made with eggs — c**u**st**a**rd
12. to stop something from happening — pr**e**v**e**nt
13. go away — d**i**s**a**pp**e**ar
14. to say you are sorry — **a**p**o**l**o**g**i**ze
15. something that breaks easily — fr**a**g**i**le
16. something not finished — **i**nc**o**mpl**e**te

60

Page 61

Use what you know about trading and regrouping to solve these problems. Use the place-value charts to help you.

EXAMPLE:

	H	T	O		H	T	O		H	T	O
1. ⁶⁹¹³7̶9̶0̶ - 289	6	10	13	b.	6	9	13	c.	5	9	10
414											

| 924 - 369 | ◯ | 8 | 11 | 14 | | 9 | 11 | 10 | | 8 | 10 | 14 |
| 254 | | | | | | | | | | | |

| 900 - 576 | ◯ | 8 | 9 | 10 | | 9 | 11 | 10 | | 8 | 10 | 14 |

| 661 - 287 | a | 5 | 16 | 11 | ◯ | 5 | 15 | 11 | c. | 6 | 6 | 11 |

Which two words make up each contraction, or what contraction comes from the two words?

1. Write the contractions for these words.
   we are — **we're**   was not — **wasn't**
   were not — **weren't**   would not — **wouldn't**

2. Write the two words in these contractions.
   they've — **they have**   should not — **should not**
   they'll — **they will**   I'd — **I would or I had**

3. Write the contractions for these words.
   he is — **he's**   she is — **she's**
   he has — **he's**   she has — **she's**

4. Write the contractions for these words.
   let us — **let's**   will not — **won't**
   does not — **doesn't**   we have — **we've**

61

Page 62

Read the directions in the box. Draw a line under the answer to each question.

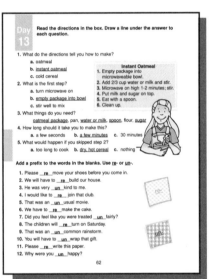

1. What do the directions tell you how to make?
   a. oatmeal
   b. <u>instant oatmeal</u>
   c. cold cereal

2. What is the first step?
   a. turn microwave on
   b. <u>empty package into bowl</u>
   c. stir well to mix

3. What things do you need?
   <u>oatmeal package, pan, water or milk, spoon, flour, sugar</u>

4. How long should it take you to make this?
   a. a few seconds   b. <u>a few minutes</u>   c. 30 minutes

5. What would happen if you skipped step 2?
   a. too long to cook   b. <u>dry, hot cereal</u>   c. nothing

Instant Oatmeal
1. Empty package into microwaveable bowl.
2. Add 2/3 cup water or milk and stir.
3. Microwave on high 1-2 minutes; stir.
4. Put milk and sugar on top.
5. Eat with a spoon.
6. Clean up.

Add a prefix to the words in the blanks. Use re- or un-.

1. Please **re** move your shoes before you come in.
2. We will have to **re** build our house.
3. He was very **un** kind to me.
4. I would like to **re** join that club.
5. That was an **un** usual movie.
6. We have to **re** make the cake.
7. Did you feel like you were treated **un** fairly?
8. The children will **re** turn on Saturday.
9. That was an **un** common rainstorm.
10. You will have to **un** wrap that gift.
11. Please **re** write this paper.
12. Why were you **un** happy?

62

Page 63

Practice finding the differences.

Ex. 5 10 6̶0̶3̶ - 240 363	300 - 130 170	510 - 250 260	804 - 163 641	905 - 662 243	404 - 142 262
4̶9̶0̶0̶ - 246 254	623 - 257 366	771 - 704 67	900 - 156 744	435 - 297 138	500 - 297 203
Ex. $7̶5̶0̶ - 6.75 $2.75	$5.00 - 1.62 $3.38	$6.15 - 4.38 $1.77	$10.32 - 7.75 $2.57	$4.06 - 1.67 $2.39	$1.00 - .67 $.33

Write, in cursive, a sentence for each of the -es words in the box.

1. **Answers will vary.**

| hooves |
| shelves |
| wolves |
| lives |
| leaves |
| scarves |
| wives |
| knives |

63

Page 64

Look at this table of contents and answer the questions.

Table of Contents	
Communicating with Others	9
Writing a Story	16
Word Meanings	20
Following Directions	25
Using Words Correctly	32
Commas	40
Proofreading	53
Describing Words	57

1. What chapters should you read to learn how to write a story? **Writing a story Proofreading**
2. On what page should you start reading to learn about commas? **Page 40**
3. How many chapters does this table of contents show? **Eight**
4. On which page would you find information on describing what something looks like? **Page 57**
5. In what chapter could you find out how to use a telephone? **Chapter 1**
6. Which chapter might tell you how to make a paper airplane? **Chapter 4**

Read the paragraph and add the correct punctuation.

Where did you go yesterday Tanner asked Denise I went to the fair she told him I will draw a picture for you She then told him about the watermelon-eating contest and the blue ribbon she won She told him about seeing pigs and prize-winning sheep It sounds like you had a fun day Denise I wish I had been with you said Tanner

Now draw a picture of something else Denise may have seen at the fair.

Pictures will vary.

64

Page 65

Read and solve the problems.

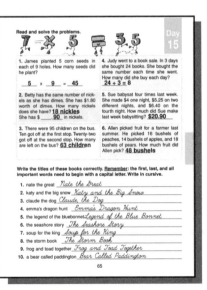

1. James planted 5 corn seeds in each of 9 holes. How many seeds did he plant?
   5 x **9** = **45**

2. Betty has the same number of nickels as she has dimes. She has $1.80 worth of dimes. How many nickels does she have? **18 nickles**
   She has $ **.90** in nickels.

3. There were 95 children on the bus. Ten got off at the first stop. Twenty-two got off at the second stop. How many are left on the bus? **63 children**

4. Judy went to a book sale. In 3 days she bought 24 books. She bought the same number each time she went. How many did she buy each day?
   24 ÷ 3 = 8

5. Sue babysat four times last week. She made $4 one night, $5.25 on two different nights, and $6.40 on the fourth night. How much did Sue make last week babysitting? **$20.90**

6. Allen picked fruit for a farmer last summer. He picked 16 bushels of peaches, 14 bushels of apples, and 18 bushels of pears. How much fruit did Allen pick? **48 bushels**

Write the titles of these books correctly. Remember: the first, last, and all important words need to begin with a capital letter. Write in cursive.

1. nate the great — *Nate the Great*
2. katy and the big snow — *Katy and the Big Snow*
3. claude the dog — *Claude, the Dog*
4. emma's dragon hunt — *Emma's Dragon Hunt*
5. the legend of the bluebonnet — *Legend of the Blue Bonnet*
6. the seashore story — *The Seashore Story*
7. soup for the king — *Soup for the King*
8. the storm book — *The Storm Book*
9. frog and toad together — *Frog and Toad Together*
10. a bear called paddington — *Bear Called Paddington*

65

Page 66

Finish writing this story.

The group of hikers did not know how long it had been since anyone had seen Don. "I know he was here just a little while ago," said Fred. Fred had said that two hours ago. There were already search parties out looking for Don.

"Don is a good hiker and should be able to find his way down the mountain," his father was saying. "But maybe he has been hurt," replied Don's friend, Craig.

Answers will vary.

Try making a comparison with nature or something else.

EXAMPLE: The first daffodils were as yellow as ___lemons___

1. The piano keys were as white as **Answers will vary.**
2. The new leaves on the trees in spring are as green as ___
3. My new sweater was as blue as the summer ___
4. That horse is as black as a dark ___
5. The fireworks were as bright as the ___
6. Her eyes were as green as the ___
7. The balloons reminded me of a bunch of ___
8. That house was as tall as a steep ___
9. The wind between my toes was as brown as ___
10. The sunset was as red and orange as ___
11. The rings on her fingers sparkled like ___
12. The bread we were trying to eat was as hard as a ___
13. I was so tired, my pillow felt as soft as a ___
14. The wind was as gentle as ___

66

Page 67

Count the money.

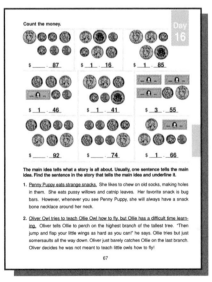

$ __.87 $ 1.16 $ 1.85

$ 1.46 $ 1.41 $ 3.55

$ __.92 $ __.74 $ 1.66

The main idea tells what a story is all about. Usually, one sentence tells the main idea. Find the sentence in the story that tells the main idea and underline it.

1. <u>Penny Puppy eats strange snacks.</u> She likes to chew on old socks, making holes in them. She eats pussy willows and catnip leaves. Her favorite snack is bug bars. However, whenever you see Penny Puppy, she will always have a snack bone necklace around her neck.

2. <u>Oliver Owl tries to teach Ollie Owl how to fly, but Ollie has a difficult time learning.</u> Oliver tells Ollie to perch on the highest branch of the tallest tree. "Then jump and flap your little wings as hard as you can!" he says. Ollie tries but just somersaults all the way down. Oliver barely catches Ollie on the last branch. Oliver decides he was not meant to teach little owls how to fly!

67

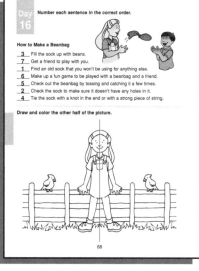

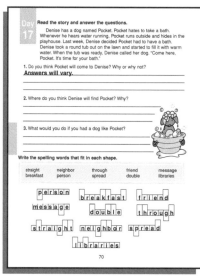
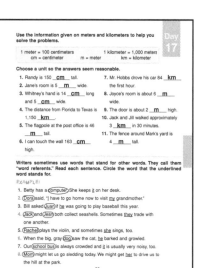
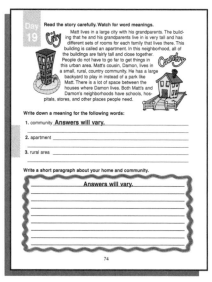
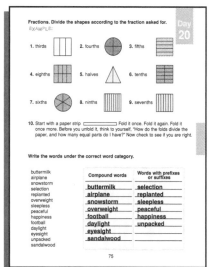
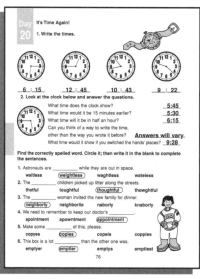

Section 3

Counting Change.

Day 1

Spent	Gave clerk	How much change?		Spent	Gave clerk	How much change?
EXAMPLE $1.35	$1.50	$.15		$9.35	$20.00	$10.65
$2.50	$5.00	$2.50		$5.55	$6.00	$.45
$.95	$1.00	$.05		$13.95	$20.00	$6.05
$1.80	$2.00	$.20		$85.00	$100.00	$15.00
$6.42	$10.00	$3.58		$100.60	$105.00	$4.40

Have you seen a parade this summer? If so, write about it. If not, make up a story about a circus parade. Give it a title. Write in cursive.

Stories will vary.

81

Day 1 **Fill in the blanks.**

Word Box
minerals
pedal
vitamins
yogurt
meter
costume
squeeze
tales
possible
public
flight
ambition
community
thigh

1. Be sure to put some money in the **meter**.
2. The **pedal** on his bike was broken.
3. For good eyesight and strong teeth, we need plenty of **vitamins**.
4. **yogurt** is made from milk.
5. The **public** did not like his speech.
6. We also need **minerals** to help us stay healthy.
7. Do you ever go to the **community** center?
8. My family took a **flight** to England.
9. I will **squeeze** some oranges for my juice.
10. My **ambition** is to become a doctor.
11. Do you like to read **tales** ?
12. Jim got a deep cut on his **thigh**.
13. What **costume** will you wear to the party?
14. Would it be **possible** for me to become president?

Stressed Syllables. The "stressed" syllable is said with a little more force than the others. Circle the stressed syllable in each of the following words. Use a dictionary if you need help. In a dictionary, the stressed syllable is preceded or followed by an accent mark.

es cape´ es (cape)

1. (doc) tor
2. (gar) den
3. re (sult)
4. (es) ca la tor
5. con (fus) ing
6. com (plete)
7. (man) age
8. con (tain) er
9. (fac) to ry
10. oc (ca) sion
11. (mess) en ger
12. un (til)
13. (li) ons
14. (char) ac ter
15. de (fective)
16. (mead) ow
17. sur (prise)
18. (daugh) ter
19. at (ten) tion
20. (rock) et

82

Multiplication and division facts are related.

Day 2

6 x 3 = 18   3 x 6 = 18   18 ÷ 3 = 6   18 ÷ 6 = 3

Use what you know to write the related facts for each problem.

5 x 3 = **15**
3 x **5** = **15**
15 ÷ **3** = **5**
15 ÷ 5 = **3**

9 x 2 = **18**
2 x **9** = **18**
18 ÷ 2 = **9**
18 ÷ 9 = **2**

7 x 3 = **21**
3 x **7** = **21**
21 ÷ 3 = **7**
21 ÷ **7** = **3**

4 x 3 = **12**
3 x **4** = **12**
12 ÷ 3 = **4**
12 ÷ 4 = **3**

6 x 4 = **24**
4 x **6** = **24**
24 ÷ **6** = **4**
24 ÷ 4 = **6**

4 x 8 = **32**
8 x **4** = **32**
32 ÷ **4** = **8**
32 ÷ 8 = **4**

7 x 5 = **30**
6 x **5** = **30**
30 ÷ **5** = **6**
30 ÷ 6 = **5**

9 x 4 = **36**
4 x **9** = **36**
36 ÷ **4** = **9**
36 ÷ 9 = **4**

Make up one of your own.   ___ x ___ = ___   **Answers will vary.**   ___ x ___ = ___   ___ ÷ ___ = ___   ___ ÷ ___ = ___

Look at the first word in each row; then find the words in the row that have the same vowel sound. Circle them.
(Hint: They do not need to have the same vowels.)

1. noise — (joy) choose (choice) (boy) know bought (voice)
2. wrote — frog (both) (coat) know bought (grow)
3. book — choose (look) (foot) spoon tooth (hook)
4. there — (bear) hair (share) near bread (spare)
5. large — (star) yard scare (mark) guard (far)
6. proud — slow (crowd) (now) (ouch) (shout) round
7. taste — (eight) white (wait) height (paint) (ate)
8. work — (world) store short (word) stork fourth

83

Day 2 **Choose the correct meaning for each word.**

Now write your own meaning for these words:

1. shine
Answers will vary.
2. dream
3. different
4. bored
5. weird

4 stick
8 choice
9 nickel
14 neat
12 pretend
7 rug
5 waste
1 center
3 trap
2 spring
10 crack
15 quiet
11 stork
13 neighbors
6 done

1. the very middle
2. sudden, upward movement
3. to catch and hold
4. thin piece of wood
5. use foolishly
6. finished
7. floor covering
8. right to choose
9. a coin
10. small break
11. large bird
12. make-believe
13. people who live near
14. good order
15. very little noise

Number these sentences in the correct order.

7 Off to the moon went Joan!
1 Joan found an old tuna can.
4 Joan told the strange animal she wanted a trip to the moon.
2 She washed the tuna can in the creek.
5 The animal said it would send her to the moon if she gave it a pair of pink rollerblades.
3 A strange animal appeared and told her she could have a wish.
6 Joan got the rollerblades and gave them to the strange animal.

Draw the strange animal.

Pictures will vary.

84

Division: There are two ways of writing it.

Day 3

1. 18 ÷ 3 = **6**
2. 24 ÷ 4 = **6**
3. 10 ÷ 2 = **5**
4. 21 ÷ 3 = **7**
5. 36 ÷ 4 = **9**
6. 32 ÷ 8 = **4**
7. 18 ÷ 3 = **6**
8. 45 ÷ 5 = **9**
9. 48 ÷ 6 = **8**
10. 42 ÷ 7 = **6**

11. 5)40 → **8**
12. 9)36 → **4**
13. 4)12 → **3**
14. 7)56 → **8**
15. 4)16 → **4**

16. 6)36 → **6**
17. 8)40 → **5**
18. 9)27 → **3**
19. 6)42 → **7**
20. 7)35 → **5**

Some verbs show present tense, some show past tense, and some need a helping verb. Example: go, give, take = present. Did, went, ran = past. Done and gone need helpers. Underline the verb and then write if it is present, past, or has a helper.

EXAMPLE

1. Mom was in a good mood.   *past*
2. I broke my mother's favorite vase yesterday.   **past**
3. Mr. Peep has given that talk many times.   **helper, has**
4. I will run down the hill with you.   **present**
5. Her mom can take us to the ball game.   **present**
6. Jane did the dishes by herself.   **past**
7. You have gone to this school for five years.   **helper, have**
8. Will you give me the money now?   **present**
9. Here! I will give it to you.   **present**
10. Let's go over to your house.   **present**

85

Day 3 **Batter Up, Batter Up**

J. J. stepped up to the plate and waited for the pitcher to throw the ball. The pitcher pitched the ball too high, but J. J. swung at it anyway. The next ball was pitched right down the center. It was so fast, J. J. missed it completely. It was not his day. The other team's fans hooted when the pitcher struck him out. He felt bad. His feelings were hurt because some people laughed at him. He also felt he had let his teammates down. He was not a quitter, though.

Write down what you think happened or should happen next with J. J. and his team.

Answers will vary.

Read the words in each group. List what you think comes first, second, and third.

2 time school's out
1 summertime is the
3 and vacations begin

3 and get tan in the sun
2 the sprinklers
1 let's run through

2 for Father's Day
3 and sunshine
1 June is the time

3 Independence Day is
2 always, always on the
1 fourth of July

3 Little Lost River
1 my family always
2 goes fishing on

3 ice cream are summer foods
2 baked beans, and
1 hot dogs, potato chips,

86

Money Matters.

Day 4

1. How much money is shown? $ **1** . **47**
2. How much money is shown? $ **1** . **86**
3. How much money is shown? $ **2** . **60**
4. Circle the largest amount of money.
   a. 60 nickels
   b. 21 dimes
   c. 99 pennies
   d. 10 quarters
5. Circle the least amount of money.
   a. 12 quarters and 1 nickel
   b. one dollar and 3 quarters
   c. 2 dollars and 5 dimes
   d. one dollar and 6 nickels

Do you remember the parts of a friendly letter?

Label the parts of this letter.

Body
Closing
Greeting
Signature
Heading

1921 King Street
Heading Boise, Idaho
August 2, 1993

Dear Sara, **Greeting**

Body { I am having a great time at camp. I swim every day and hike a lot, too. Yesterday, our group hiked five miles.

I hope you are feeling better.

Closing Your friend,
Signature Bugs

87

Day 4 **Cause and Effect.**
Read the sentences; then circle the effect, the part that tells what happened. Underline the cause, the part that tells why it happened.

EXAMPLE: The sky became cloudy, and then it started to snow.

1. The cold weather caused frost to cover the windows.
2. The falling snowflakes made my cheeks wet and cold.
3. Snow stuck to my mittens because I had made a snowman.
4. The snowman melted from the heat of the sun.
5. I played so long in the sun, I got a bad sunburn.
6. Pinocchio's nose grew longer every time he told a lie.
7. Snow White woke up when the prince kissed her.
8. The lady went to the well to get a bucket of water.
9. Our big oak tree was blown down by a strong wind.
10. Miss Mouse got very fat because she ate so much cheese.
11. The policeman gave Dad a ticket because he was going too fast.
12. We had to play in the house because it was raining hard.

Pretend this island is out in the ocean. Answer the questions about it.

Pint Island

1. Which river runs into Lake Ho? **L. River**
2. Which ocean is south of the island? **Cary Ocean**
3. How many mountain ranges are there? **two**
4. Which river is the longest? **T. River**
5. What ocean is north of Pint Island? **Chick Ocean**
6. What is the name of the capital city? **Peek City**
7. What direction is Hi Town from Toe Town? **South**

88

Page 89

Division.

$7\overline{)56}$ → **8** $7\overline{)28}$ → **4** $8\overline{)32}$ → **4** $8\overline{)48}$ → **6**

$6\overline{)54}$ → **9** $5\overline{)35}$ → **7** $7\overline{)42}$ → **6** $9\overline{)45}$ → **5**

$6\overline{)18}$ → **3** $7\overline{)49}$ → **7** $9\overline{)81}$ → **9** $6\overline{)36}$ → **6**

$8\overline{)72}$ → **9** $9\overline{)27}$ → **3** $9\overline{)63}$ → **7** $8\overline{)40}$ → **5**

$24 \div 6 =$ **4** $63 \div 7 =$ **9** $25 \div 5 =$ **5**

$12 \div 4 =$ **3** $72 \div 9 =$ **8** $28 \div 7 =$ **4**

$42 \div 6 =$ **7** $30 \div 5 =$ **6** $56 \div 8 =$ **7**

Circle the pronouns in the sentences. <u>Remember</u>: Pronouns take the place of a noun. There can be more than one in some sentences.

1. I told (her) about Val's horse.
2. This piece of cake is for (him).
3. Liz invited Joe and (me) to the party.
4. The table is all set for (us).
5. (We) are too late to see the first show.
6. (They) will be happy to come with (us).
7. Ray caught two bugs, and later (he) freed them.
8. This pie is for (you) and (me) to eat for dessert.
9. Lisa had a hard time doing the test, but (it) is over now.
10. Clams and turtles have shells. (They) are protected by (them).
11. (He) is Jan's best friend.
12. (They) have been best friends for a long time.
13. Can (you) find the Big Dipper in the sky?
14. (My) camera was broken, but Dad fixed it.

89

Page 90

Unscramble the words and write them correctly in the blanks to complete the sentences.

1. Pillows are to <u>soft</u> as boards are to **hard** . rdha
2. Oranges are to <u>juicy</u> as crackers are to **dry** . dyr
3. Braces are to <u>teeth</u> as glasses are to **eyes** . esey
4. Bells are to <u>ring</u> as cars are to **honk** . nkho
5. Hear is to <u>ears</u> as touch is to **fingers** . serinfg
6. Shout is to <u>noise</u> as whisper is to **quiet** . uetqi
7. Star is to <u>pointed</u> as circle is to **round** . dunor
8. Scaly is to <u>fish</u> as furry is to **kitten** . ttnike
9. Ant is to <u>crawl</u> as frog is to **leap** . pael
10. Elephant is to <u>large</u> as mouse is to **small** . malsl
11. Paint is to <u>brush</u> as draw is to **pencil** . cienlp
12. Buckle is to <u>belt</u> as tie is to **shoelace** . lacehoes
13. Bananas are to <u>peel</u> as eggs are to **crack** . cckra
14. Night is to <u>dark</u> as day is to **light** . htgli

Think of a story to fit the pictures. Write in the words.

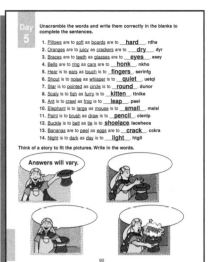

Answers will vary.

90

Page 91

Adding more than two addends.

65	22	78	51	42	87
59	46	32	26	39	32
+11	+38	+21	+26	+71	+19
135	**106**	**131**	**103**	**152**	**138**

54	38	39	43	37	17
19	22	71	36	46	19
+68	+46	+42	+18	+28	+12
141	**106**	**152**	**97**	**111**	**48**

215	325	429	742	395	
463	48	330	135	205	
+306	+113	+127	+173	+341	
984	**486**	**886**	**1050**	**941**	

Read the following words. Write down how many vowels are in each word, how many vowel sounds you hear, and how many syllables there are.

EXAMPLE:

	Number of vowels	Number of vowel sounds	Number of syllables
Afraid	3	2	2

	v	vs	syl			v	vs	syl
1. afternoon	4	3	3	8. education	5	4	4
2. formula	3	3	3	9. problem	2	2	2
3. separated	4	4	4	10. migrate	3	2	2
4. fantastic	3	3	3	11. submarine	4	3	3
5. memories	4	3	3	12. belated	3	3	3
6. experience	5	4	4	13. advertising	4	4	4
7. successful	3	3	3	14. characteristic	5	5	5

91

Page 92

Write your own ending for each sentence. Try to use more than two or three words. Write in cursive.

1. I like the flavor of **Answers will vary.**
2. My parents disapproved when I _____
3. I once read a story about a boy who became a knight because he _____
4. The rodeo started with _____
5. Richard swam over to the dock to _____
6. The kite drifted away _____
7. The baby crawled across _____
8. The long winter was beginning _____
9. It was fun to watch the rabbit nibble _____
10. The cars were piled high _____
11. Lance won a prize for _____
12. Do you like to play _____?

Can you put these puzzle pieces together and read the message? Don't cut them out. If you need more help, practice on a piece of scratch paper. The c and the m are already there to help you.

I	W	O	U	L	D
L	I	K	E	T	O
B	E	C	O	M	E
F	A	M	O	U	S
A	N	D	U	S	E
W	I	S	D	O	M

92

Page 93

Find the products.

EXAMPLE:

58	42	67	66	35	23
x3	x8	x5	x3	x6	x3
174	**336**	**335**	**198**	**210**	**69**

23	29	25	44	94	35
x9	x4	x9	x6	x2	x8
207	**116**	**225**	**264**	**188**	**280**

25	21	75	68	41	63
x4	x6	x4	x3	x7	x2
100	**126**	**300**	**204**	**287**	**126**

52	14	49	78	54	81
x4	x6	x4	x5	x8	x5
208	**84**	**196**	**390**	**432**	**405**

A pronoun showing ownership is a possessive pronoun, such as...

mine ours yours his hers theirs its their my your mine our

Write six sentences in cursive. Use a possessive pronoun in each one of them.

Answers will vary.

93

Page 94

What does the underlined phrase really mean? Circle your answer.

1. It was raining <u>cats and dogs</u>.
   a. Real cats and dogs were falling out of the sky.
   (b. It was raining very hard.)
   c. It wasn't raining at all.
2. The night was <u>black as coal</u>.
   (a. The night was very dark.)
   b. The sky was light.
   c. The night was turning into day.
3. I was so thirsty I felt like I <u>could spit cotton</u>.
   (a. My mouth was very dry.)
   b. I had cotton in my mouth.
   c. I did not need a drink.
4. The sun on the snow made it <u>sparkle like diamonds</u>.
   a. There were diamonds in the snow.
   b. The snow was dirty and dull.
   (c. The snow was clean and shiny.)
5. <u>Time flies</u> when we are having fun.
   (a. Time goes quickly.)
   b. Time has wings and flies like a bird.
   c. Time goes slowly.
6. The train <u>roared like a lion</u> as it went through the mountain pass.
   a. The train was quiet.
   b. The train has a voice.
   (c. The train was loud and fast.)
7. Andy made two <u>home runs</u> during the ball game.
   a. Andy ran home.
   (b. Andy ran around all the bases and scored.)
   c. Andy got out.
8. My sister is as <u>gentle as a lamb</u> with sick people.
   a. My sister is soft.
   b. My sister doesn't like sick people.
   (c. My sister is kind to sick people.)

94

Page 95

Find the quotients and the remainders.

EXAMPLE:

$4\overline{)26}$ → **6 R2** $3\overline{)14}$ → **4 R2** $5\overline{)39}$ → **7 R4** $3\overline{)16}$ → **5 R1** $3\overline{)23}$ → **7 R2**

$2\overline{)19}$ → **9 R1** $6\overline{)29}$ → **4 R5** $4\overline{)21}$ → **5 R1** $5\overline{)36}$ → **7 R1** $4\overline{)18}$ → **4 R2**

$5\overline{)34}$ → **6 R4** $4\overline{)22}$ → **5 R2** $5\overline{)42}$ → **8 R2** $4\overline{)33}$ → **8 R1** $5\overline{)27}$ → **5 R2**

$2\overline{)84}$ → **42** $3\overline{)60}$ → **20** $4\overline{)68}$ → **17** $4\overline{)96}$ → **24** $5\overline{)80}$ → **16**

$3\overline{)93}$ → **31** $4\overline{)76}$ → **19** $2\overline{)90}$ → **45** $4\overline{)44}$ → **11** $4\overline{)72}$ → **18**

$2\overline{)50}$ → **25** $3\overline{)84}$ → **28** $3\overline{)78}$ → **26** $4\overline{)56}$ → **14** $4\overline{)68}$ → **17**

Cursive writing review. School starts soon, so remember to...

1. Make each letter smooth and clear.
2. Space letters evenly.
3. Make each letter the correct shape and size.
4. Make each letter touch the line correctly.
5. Make your letters slant in the same direction.

Copy the following statement, or do one of your own! I love to practice writing in cursive. It makes me feel very grown-up!

Answers will vary.

95

Page 96

Get a dictionary and look up the following words and write the special spelling for each word in the blank provided. Put in all the markings.

EXAMPLE: magnolia măg nōl´ yə. **Remember:** The special spelling tells you how to say a word correctly, how many syllables there are, where they are divided, and which syllable is stressed.

1. porcupine   pôr´ kyoo - pin´
2. electromagnet   ĭ - lek´ trō - mag´ nit
3. elate   ĭ - lāt´
4. gravity   grav´ ə - tĭ
5. labor   lā´ bər
6. cupboard   kŭb´ ə rd
7. chisel   chĭz´ l
8. testify   test´ təfī´
9. nitrate   nī´trāt
10. violinist   vī´ə l - in - ist

Choose three words from above and write their meaning.

1. word _____ meaning **Answers will vary.**
2. word _____ meaning
3. word _____ meaning

We taste things because of our tongue and nose. The smell helps our tongue taste things. Ask your parents if you can taste some foods you have in your house. Tell whether they are bitter, sour, sweet, or salty. Write the name of the food you tasted under the correct heading.

EXAMPLE:

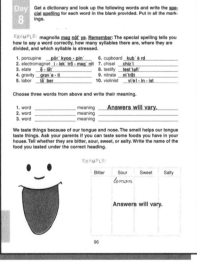

Bitter	Sour	Sweet	Salty
	lemon		
	Answers will vary.		

96

Page 97

Complete the times table wheels.

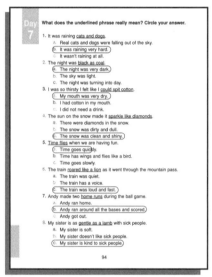

Underline the base or root word in each compound word.

blossoms   immediately   wreckage   incorrect
misspelled   inspector   retrace   reappear
exporting   invention   exhausted   messages

Underline the prefix in each word.

unusual   microphone   submarine   disappoint
displeased   invisible   extend   misplace
defrost   encircle   recover   enlarge

Underline the suffix in each word.

happiness   silently   tiniest   potatoes
hesitated   pleasantly   hasty   scarcely
mouthful   careless   graceful   spelling

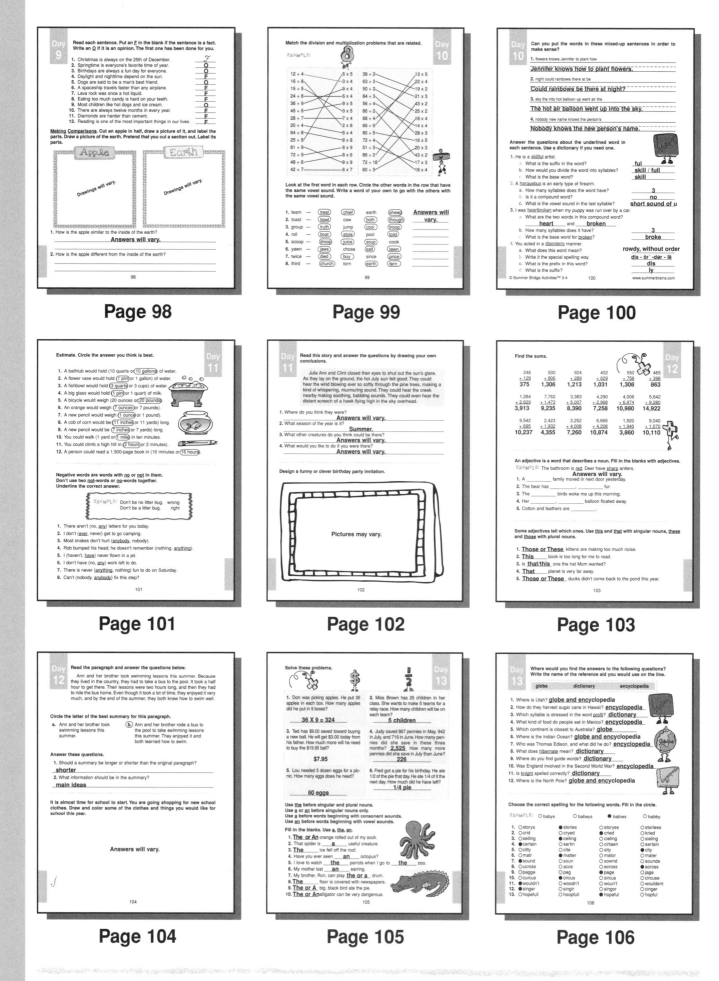

Page 98

Page 99

Page 100

Page 101

Page 102

Page 103

Page 104

Page 105

Page 106

Page 107

Do these problems. Be sure to look at the signs. Use a calculator to help you if you have one.

25 - 5 = **20**   28 ÷ 4 = **7**   11 x 11 = **121**
6 x 1 = **6**   14 ÷ 7 = **2**   36 - 16 = **20**
36 ÷ 6 = **6**   16 ÷ 6 = **22**   18 ÷ 3 = **6**
5 x 6 = **30**   18 - 8 = **10**   9 x 2 = **18**
17 ÷ 3 = **20** 10 x 3 = **30**   7 x 7 = **49**
11 ÷ 8 = **19** 7 - 3 = **4**   81 ÷ 9 = **9**
19 - 4 = **15** 22 - 2 = **20**   24 ÷ 12 = **36**
4 x 2 = **8**   7 x 6 = **42**   54 ÷ 9 = **6**
9 ÷ 3 = **3**   3 x 7 = **21**   93 - 10 = **83**
12 ÷ 3 = **4**   84 - 80 = **4**   6 x 8 = **48**
4 ÷ 4 = **8**   2 x 10 = **20**   9 ÷ 6 = **15**
10 ÷ 5 = **2**   12 - 6 = **6**   10 x 10 = **100**

Here are some more spelling words. Practice writing them in cursive. Then have someone give you a test on them. Use another piece of paper.

probably	*probably*
sincerely	*sincerely*
minute	*minute*
guest	*guest*
similar	*similar*
remember	*remember*
smooth	*smooth*
garage	*garage*
living	*living*
jeans	*jeans*
once	*once*
knobby	*knobby*

107

Page 108

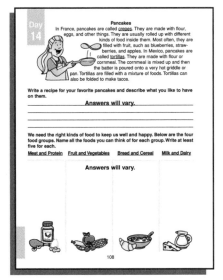

Pancakes

In France, pancakes are called crepes. They are made with flour, eggs, and other things. They are usually rolled up with different kinds of food inside them. Most often, they are filled with fruit, such as blueberries, straw-berries, and apples. In Mexico, pancakes are called tortillas. They are made with flour or cornmeal. The cornmeal is mixed up and then the batter is poured onto a very hot griddle or pan. Tortillas are filled with a mixture of foods. Tortillas can also be folded to make tacos.

Write a recipe for your favorite pancakes and describe what you like to have on them.

Answers will vary.

We need the right kinds of food to keep us well and happy. Below are the four food groups. Name all the foods you can think of for each group. Write at least five for each.

Meat and Protein	Fruit and Vegetables	Bread and Cereal	Milk and Dairy
	Answers will vary.		

108

Page 109

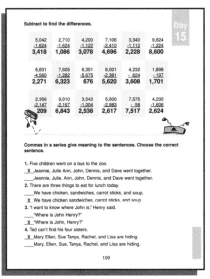

Subtract to find the differences.

5,042	2,710	4,200	7,106	3,340	9,824
-1,624	-1,624	-1,122	-2,410	-1,112	-1,224
3,418	**1,086**	**3,078**	**4,696**	**2,228**	**8,600**

6,831	7,605	6,351	8,001	4,232	1,898
-4,560	-1,282	-5,675	-2,381	- 624	- 197
2,271	**6,323**	**676**	**5,620**	**3,608**	**1,701**

2,356	9,010	3,542	5,600	7,575	4,230
-2,147	-2,167	-1,004	-2,983	- 58	-1,606
209	**6,843**	**2,538**	**2,617**	**7,517**	**2,624**

Commas in a series give meaning to the sentences. Choose the correct sentence.

1. Five children went on a bus to the zoo.
_____ Jeannie, Julie Ann, John, Dennis, and Dave went together.
__X__ Jeannie, Julie, Ann, John, Dennis, and Dave went together.

2. There are three things to eat for lunch today.
_____ We have chicken, sandwiches, carrot sticks, and soup.
__X__ We have chicken sandwiches, carrot sticks, and soup.

3. "I want to know where John is," Henry said.
_____ "Where is John Henry?"
__X__ "Where is John, Henry?"

4. Ted can't find his four sisters.
__X__ Mary Ellen, Sue Tanya, Rachel, and Lisa are hiding.
_____ Mary, Ellen, Sue, Tanya, Rachel, and Lisa are hiding.

109

Page 110

Read the main idea sentence and the details below. Put an X before each detail important to the main idea.

One Saturday, Mike took his little sister, Judy, for a walk.

__X__ They walked around the paths of the big housing project.

_____ There, on a weed, was a big, fat, green caterpillar.

__X__ They knew they mustn't walk on the fresh, green grass of the lawns.

_____ They could hunt under the hedges along the walks for beetles, ants, and earthworms.

_____ They showed their friend, Jake, the caterpillar.

Look at these words and use them to fill in the blanks.

enough	tube	brought	fantastic
where	woman	through	daughter

1. Which word ends with the same sound as lipstick? **fantastic**

2. Which word rhymes with ought? **brought**

3. Which word begins the same as what? **where**

4. Which word has the same vowel sound as too? **tube**

5. Write the spelling words that make a pair.
son **daughter** man **woman**

6. Write the spelling word that ends with the same sound as off.
enough

7. What word ends with the same sound as chew? **through**

110

Notes

_____
_____
_____
_____
_____
_____
_____
_____
_____
_____
_____
_____
_____
_____
_____
_____
_____
_____
_____

5 Five things I'm thankful for:

1. _____
2. _____
3. _____
4. _____
5. _____

Better Bodies   Better Behavior

Up until now, Summer Bridge Activities has been all about your mind…

But the other parts of you—who you are, how you act, and how you feel—are important too. That's why this year we are introducing a whole new section in Summer Bridge Activities: Building Better Bodies and Behavior. These new pages are all about helping build a better you this summer.

Keeping your body strong and healthy helps you live better, learn better, and feel better. To keep your body healthy, you need to do things like eat right, get enough sleep, and exercise. The Physical Fitness pages of Building Better Bodies will teach you about good eating habits and the importance of proper exercise. You can even train for a Presidential Fitness Award over the summer.

The Character pages are all about building a better you on the inside. They've got fun activities for you and your family to do together. The activities will help you develop important values and habits you'll need as you grow up.

After a summer of Building Better Bodies and Behavior and Summer Bridge Activities, there may be a whole new you ready for school in the fall!

● ●

For Parents: Introduction to Character Education

Character education is simply giving your child clear messages about the values you and your family consider important. Many studies have shown that a basic core of values is universal. You will find certain values reflected in the laws of every country and incorporated in the teachings of religious, ethical, and other belief systems throughout the world.

The character activities included here are designed to span the entire summer. Each week your child will be introduced to a new value, with a quote and two activities that illustrate it. Research has shown that character education is most effective when parents reinforce the values in their child's daily routine; therefore, we encourage parents to be involved as their child completes the lessons.

Here are some suggestions on how to maximize these lessons.
- Read through the lesson yourself. Then set aside a block of time when you and your child discuss the value.
- Plan a block of time to work on the suggested activities.
- Discuss the meaning of the quote with your child. Ask, "What do you think the quote means?" Have your child ask other members of the family the same question. If possible, include grandparents, aunts, uncles, and cousins.

- Use the quote as often as you can during the week. You'll be pleasantly surprised to learn that both you and your child will have it memorized.
- For extra motivation, you can set a reward for completing each week's activities.
- Point out to your child other people who are actively displaying a value. Example: "See how John is helping Mrs. Olsen by raking her leaves."
- Be sure to praise your child each time he or she practices a value: "Mary, it was very courteous of you to wait until I finished speaking."
- Find time in your day to talk about values. Turn off the radio in the car and chat with your children; take a walk in the evening as a family; read a story about the weekly value at bedtime; or give a back rub while you talk about what makes your child happy or sad.
- Finally, model the values you want your child to acquire. Remember, children will do as you do, not as you say.

How I Measure Up!

Name _____   Date _____

You will be filling out this page twice—once now and once at the end of the summer to see how you have grown. Have someone help you measure yourself to fill in the blanks below. Write your answers in inches.

around the neck ___ / ___

neck to belly button ___ / ___

around the wrist ___ / ___

waist to ankle ___ / ___

foot length ___ / ___

smile ___ / ___

shoulder to elbow ___ / ___

elbow to wrist ___ / ___

around the waist ___ / ___

length of longest finger ___ / ___

around the knee ___ / ___

around the ankle ___ / ___

length of longest finger ___ / ___

around the wrist ___ / ___

around the neck ___ / ___

neck to belly button ___ / ___

around the waist ___ / ___

waist to ankle ___ / ___

foot length ___ / ___

smile ___ / ___

shoulder to elbow ___ / ___

elbow to wrist ___ / ___

around the knee ___ / ___

around the ankle ___ / ___

Building Better Bodies and Behavior   128   © Summer Bridge Activities™

Nutrition

The food you eat helps your body grow and gives you energy to work and play. Some foods give you protein or fats. Other foods provide vitamins, minerals, or carbohydrates. These are all things your body needs. Eating lots of different foods from the five major food groups every day can help you stay healthy.

Each day your body needs several servings of food from each group:

What foods did you eat today?

Which food group did you eat the most foods from today?

From which food group did you eat the least?

Which meal included the most food groups?

Meal Planning

Plan out three balanced meals for one day. Arrange your meals so that by the end of the day, you will have had all the recommended servings of the food groups listed on the Food Pyramid.

Breakfast

_____

_____

_____

_____

_____

Lunch

_____

_____

_____

_____

_____

Dinner

_____

_____

_____

_____

_____

Meal Tracker

Use these charts to record the servings from each food group you eat for one or two weeks. Have another family member keep track, too, and compare.

	Breads / Cereals	Milk	Meat	Fruits	Vegetables	Fats/Sweets
Monday						
Tuesday						
Wednesday						
Thursday						
Friday						
Saturday						
Sunday						

	Breads / Cereals	Milk	Meat	Fruits	Vegetables	Fats/Sweets
Monday						
Tuesday						
Wednesday						
Thursday						
Friday						
Saturday						
Sunday						

	Breads / Cereals	Milk	Meat	Fruits	Vegetables	Fats/Sweets
Monday						
Tuesday						
Wednesday						
Thursday						
Friday						
Saturday						
Sunday						

	Breads / Cereals	Milk	Meat	Fruits	Vegetables	Fats/Sweets
Monday						
Tuesday						
Wednesday						
Thursday						
Friday						
Saturday						
Sunday						

Get Moving!

**Did you know that getting no exercise can be almost as bad for you as smoking?!
So get moving this summer!**

Summer is the perfect time to get out and get in shape. Your fitness program should include three parts:

• Get 30 minutes of aerobic exercise per day, three to five days a week.

• Exercise your muscles to improve strength and flexibility.

• Make it FUN! Do things that you like to do. Include your friends and family.

- -

Couch Potato Quiz

1. Name three things you do each day that get you moving.

2. Name three things you do a few times a week that are good exercise.

3. How many hours do you spend each week playing outside or exercising?

4. How much TV do you watch each day?

5. How much time do you spend playing computer or video games?

If the time you spend on activities 4 and 5 adds up to more than you spend on 1–3, you could be headed for a spud's life!

Activity Pyramid

The Activity Pyramid works like the Food Pyramid. You can use the Activity Pyramid to help plan your summer exercise program. Fill in the blanks below.

List 1 thing that isn't good exercise that you could do less of this summer.

1._____

List 3 fun activities you enjoy that get you moving and are good exercise.

1._____

2._____

3._____

List 3 exercises you could do to build strength and flexibility this summer.

1._____

2._____

3._____

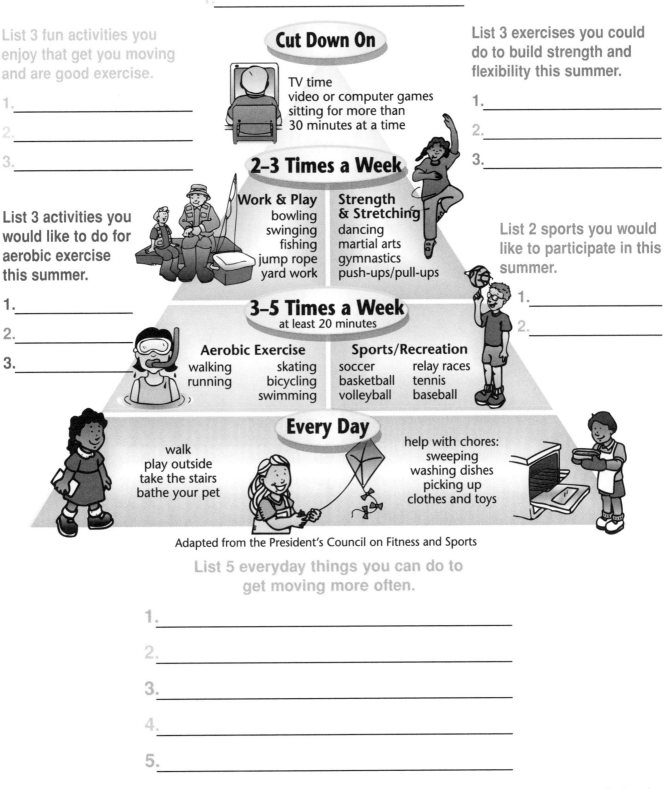

Cut Down On

TV time
video or computer games
sitting for more than
30 minutes at a time

2–3 Times a Week

Work & Play
bowling
swinging
fishing
jump rope
yard work

Strength & Stretching
dancing
martial arts
gymnastics
push-ups/pull-ups

List 3 activities you would like to do for aerobic exercise this summer.

1._____

2._____

3._____

List 2 sports you would like to participate in this summer.

1._____

2._____

3–5 Times a Week
at least 20 minutes

Aerobic Exercise
walking   skating
running   bicycling
                 swimming

Sports/Recreation
soccer   relay races
basketball   tennis
volleyball   baseball

Every Day

walk
play outside
take the stairs
bathe your pet

help with chores:
sweeping
washing dishes
picking up
clothes and toys

Adapted from the President's Council on Fitness and Sports

List 5 everyday things you can do to get moving more often.

1._____

2._____

3._____

4._____

5._____

Fitness Fundamentals

Basic physical fitness includes several things:

Cardiovascular Endurance. Your cardiovascular system includes your heart and blood vessels. You need a strong heart to pump your blood. Your blood delivers oxygen and nutrients to your body.

Muscular Strength. This is how strong your muscles are.

Muscular Endurance. Endurance has to do with how long you can use your muscles before they get tired.

Flexibility. This is your ability to move your joints and to use your muscles through their full range of motion.

Body Composition. Your body is made up of what is called lean mass and fat mass.

Lean mass includes the water, muscles, tissues, and organs in your body.

Fat mass includes the fat your body stores for energy. Exercise helps you burn body fat and maintain good body composition.

The goal of a summer fitness program is to improve in all the areas of physical fitness.

You build cardiovascular endurance through **aerobic** exercise. For **aerobic** exercise, you need to work large muscle groups at a steady pace. This increases your heart rate and breathing. You can jog, walk, hike, swim, dance, do aerobics, ride a bike, go rowing, climb stairs, rollerblade, play golf, backpack…

You should get at least 30 minutes of aerobic exercise per day, three to five days a week.

You build muscular strength and endurance with exercises that work your muscles, like sit-ups, push-ups, pull-ups, and weight lifting.

Flexibility. You can increase flexibility through stretching exercises. These are good for warm-ups too.

Find these fitness words.

Word Bank

aerobic	exercise	fat
muscular	flexible	blood
endurance	strength	oxygen
heart rate	joint	hiking

```
u a e y i d t y a g d x p o b
o l s h s t r e n g t h l r c
e w l o o o z v s d m i h d t
g t z w s j o i n t m n k a o
s q a c h i p s a d e t f f m
k c q r x i q f l e x i b l e
e e j o t v k w t e u r g e g
i e s e d r v i n t n f k x o
k e l i d c a d n n e g e j w
u z e d c y u e i g g x i c i
j c i b o r e a h h y w v s i
a m r a a c e m x x x y d i g
f p v n p n d x u s o x e f k
p o c b l o o d e g z a x m c
l e m u s c u l a r m k g i s
```

Your Summer Fitness Program

Start your summer fitness program by choosing at least one aerobic activity from your Activity Pyramid. You can choose more than one for variety.

_____   _____   _____

Do this activity three to five times each week. Keep it up for at least 20 minutes each time.
(Exercise hard enough to increase your heart rate and your breathing. But don't exercise so hard that you get dizzy or can't catch your breath.)

Use this chart to plan when you will exercise or to record your activity after you exercise.

DATE	ACTIVITY	TIME

DATE	ACTIVITY	TIME

Plan a reward for meeting your exercise goals for two weeks.
(You can make copies of this chart to track your fitness all summer long.)

Start Slow!
Remember to start out slow. Exercise is about getting stronger. It's not about being superman—or superwoman—right off the bat.

Are You Up to the Challenge?

The Presidential Physical Fitness Award Program was designed to help kids get into shape and have fun. To earn the award, you take five fitness tests. These are usually given by teachers at school, but you can train for them this summer.

Remember: Start Slow!

1. Curl-ups. Lie on the floor with your knees bent and your feet about 12 inches from your buttocks. Cross your arms over your chest. Raise your trunk up and touch your elbows to your thighs. Do as many as you can in one minute.

2. Shuttle Run. Draw a starting line. Put two blocks 30 feet away. Run the 30 feet, pick up a block, and bring it back to the starting line. Then run and bring back the second block. Record your fastest time.

3. V-sit Reach. Sit on the floor with your legs straight and your feet 8 to 12 inches apart. Put a ruler between your feet, pointing past your toes. Have a partner hold your legs straight, and keep your toes pointed up. Link your thumbs together and reach forward, palms down, as far as you can along the ruler.

4. One-Mile Walk/Run. On a track or some safe area, run one mile. You can walk as often as you need to. Finish as fast as possible. (Ages six to seven may want to run a quarter mile; ages eight to nine, half a mile.)

5. Pull-ups. Grip a bar with an overhand grip (the backs of your hands toward your face). Have someone lift you up if you need help. Hang with your arms and legs straight. Pull your body up until your chin is over the bar; then let yourself back down. Do as many as you can.

Make a chart to track your progress. Keep working all summer to see if you can improve your score.

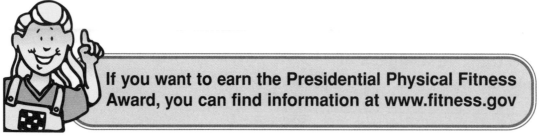

If you want to earn the Presidential Physical Fitness Award, you can find information at www.fitness.gov

Respect

Respect is showing good manners toward all people, not just those you know or who are like you. Respect is treating everyone, no matter what religion, race, or culture, male or female, rich or poor, in a way that you would want to be treated.

The easiest way to do this is to decide to **never** take part in activities and to **never** use words that make fun of people because they are different from you or your friends.

It's not necessary for eagles to be crows. What I am, I am.

~ Sitting Bull

Rob, please pass some cake.

Word Find

Find these words that also mean *respect*.

Word Bank									
	m	c	e	t	a	r	e	n	e	v
honor	w	j	t	a	h	p	s	e	p	t
idolize	e	c	a	d	n	n	t	z	i	w
admire	z	v	i	m	w	u	k	i	h	r
worship	i	e	c	i	h	b	h	n	s	o
recognize	l	z	e	r	v	b	j	g	r	n
appreciate	o	i	r	e	k	a	u	o	o	o
venerate	d	r	p	g	m	e	e	c	w	h
prize	i	p	p	b	g	c	h	e	r	j
	q	f	a	b	f	g	u	r	r	z

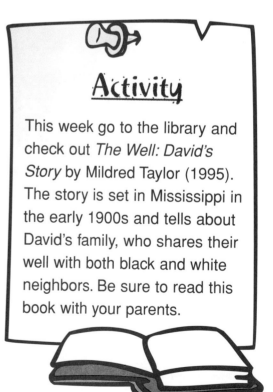

Activity

This week go to the library and check out *The Well: David's Story* by Mildred Taylor (1995). The story is set in Mississippi in the early 1900s and tells about David's family, who shares their well with both black and white neighbors. Be sure to read this book with your parents.

Gratitude

Gratitude is when you thank people for the good things they have given you or done for you. Thinking about people and events in your life that make you feel grateful (thankful) will help you become a happier person.

There are over 465 different ways of saying thank you. Here are a few:

Danke   *Toda*   *Merci*   Gracias   **Nandri**

Spasibo   Arigato   **Gadda ge**   Paldies   Hvala

Make a list of ten things you are grateful for.

1. _____
2. _____
3. _____
4. _____
5. _____

6. _____
7. _____
8. _____
9. _____
10. _____

A Recipe for Saying Thanks

1. Make a colorful card.
2. On the inside write a thank-you note to someone who has done something nice for you.
3. Address an envelope to that person.
4. Pick out a cool stamp.
5. Drop your note in the nearest mailbox.

Saying thank you creates love.

~ Daphne Rose Kingma

Courtesy

If you were the only person in the world, you wouldn't have to have **good manners** or be **courteous**. However, there are over six billion people on our planet, and good manners help us all get along with each other.

Children with good manners are usually well liked by other children and certainly by adults. Here are some simple rules for good manners:

- When you ask for something, say, "Please."
- When someone gives you something, say, "Thank you."
- When someone says, "Thank you," say, "You're welcome."
- If you walk in front of someone or bump into a person, say, "Excuse me."
- When someone else is talking, wait before speaking.
- Share and take turns.

No kindness, no matter how small, is ever wasted. ~ Aesop's Fables

Word Search. Find these words or phrases that deal with *courtesy*.

Word Bank
etiquette
thank you
welcome
excuse me
please
share
turns
patience
polite
manners

```
m u o y k n a h t
e m o c l e w e e
e s a e l p x f c
a m q u f c x r n
e t t e u q i t e
s r g s n r u t i
s r e n n a m g t
v m p o l i t e a
e i e r a h s h p
```

I've Got Manners

Make a colorful poster to display on your bedroom door or on the refrigerator. List five ways you are going to practice your manners. Be creative and decorate with watercolors, poster paints, pictures cut from magazines, clip art, or geometric shapes.

Instead of making a poster, you could make a mobile to hang from your ceiling that shows five different manners to practice.

Consequences

A consequence is what happens after you choose to do something. Some choices lead to good consequences. Other choices lead to bad consequences. An example of this would be choosing whether to eat an apple or a bag of potato chips. The potato chips might seem like a more tasty snack, but eating an apple is better for your body. Or, you may not like to do your homework, but if you choose not to, you won't do well in school, and you may not be able to go out with your friends.

It's hard to look into the future and see how a choice will influence what happens today, tomorrow, or years from now. But whenever we choose to do something, there are consequences that go with our choice. That's why it is important to *think before you choose.*

Remember: The easiest choice does not always lead to the best consequence.

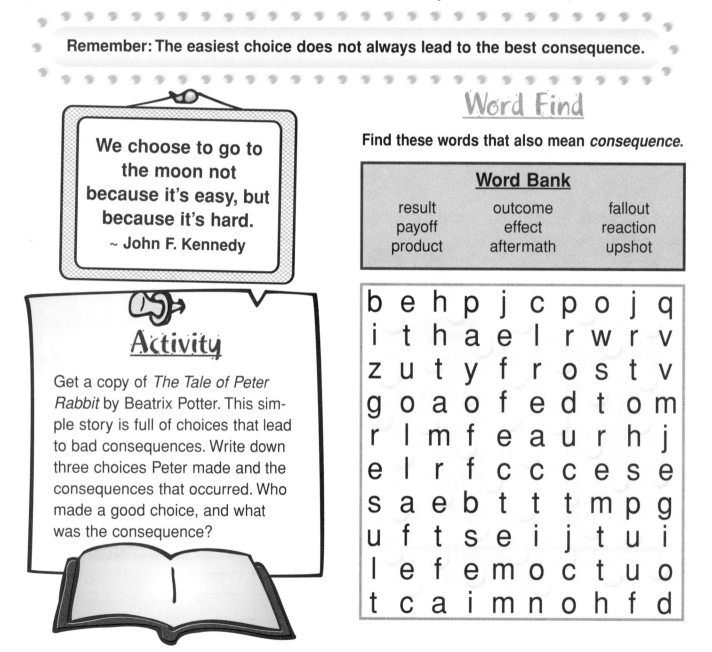

> **We choose to go to the moon not because it's easy, but because it's hard.**
> ~ John F. Kennedy

Activity

Get a copy of *The Tale of Peter Rabbit* by Beatrix Potter. This simple story is full of choices that lead to bad consequences. Write down three choices Peter made and the consequences that occurred. Who made a good choice, and what was the consequence?

Word Find

Find these words that also mean *consequence*.

Word Bank

result	outcome	fallout
payoff	effect	reaction
product	aftermath	upshot

```
b e h p j c p o j q
i t h a e l r w r v
z u t y f r o s t v
g o a o f e d t o m
r l m f e a u r h j
e l r f c c c e s e
s a e b t t t m p g
u f t s e i j t u i
l e f e m o c t u o
t c a i m n o h f d
```

Friendship

Friends come in all sizes, shapes, and ages: brothers, sisters, parents, neighbors, good teachers, and school and sports friends.

There is a saying, "To have a friend you need to be a friend." Can you think of a day when someone might have tried to get you to say or do unkind things to someone else? Sometimes it takes courage to be a real friend.

Recipe for Friendship

1 cup of always listening to ideas and stories
2 pounds of never talking behind a friend's back
1 pound of no mean teasing
2 cups of always helping a friend who needs help

Take these ingredients and mix completely together. Add laughter, kindness, hugs, and even tears. Bake for as long as it takes to make your friendship good and strong.

I get by with a little help from my friends.
~ John Lennon

Family Night at the Movies

Rent *Toy Story* or *Toy Story II*. Each movie is a simple, yet powerful, tale about true friendship. Fix a big bowl of popcorn to share with your family during the show.

International Friendship Day

The first Sunday in August is International Friendship Day. This is a perfect day to remember all your friends and how they have helped you during your friendship. Give your friends a call or send them an email or snail-mail card.

Confidence

People are **confident**, or have **confidence**, when they feel like they can succeed at a certain task. To feel confident about doing something, most people need to practice a task over and over.

Reading, pitching a baseball, writing in cursive, playing the flute, even mopping a floor are all examples of tasks that need to be practiced before people feel confident they can succeed.

What are five things you feel confident doing?

What is one thing you want to feel more confident doing?

Make a plan for how and when you will practice until you feel confident.

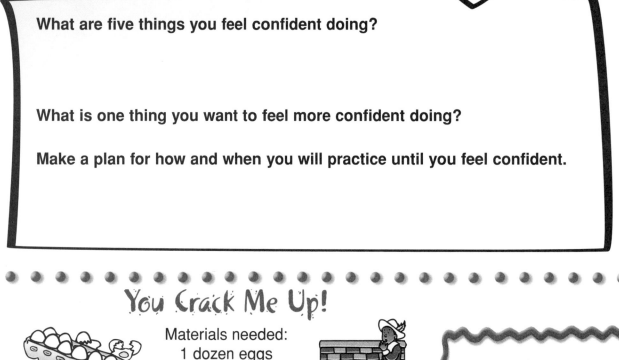

You Crack Me Up!

Materials needed:
1 dozen eggs
a mixing bowl

Cracking eggs without breaking the yolk or getting egg whites all over your hands takes practice.

1. Watch an adult break an egg into the bowl. How did they hold their hands? How did they pull the egg apart?

2. Now you try. Did you do a perfect job the first time? Keep trying until you begin to feel confident about cracking eggs.

3. Use the eggs immediately to make a cheese omelet or custard pie. Refrigerate any unused eggs for up to three days.

Pride

Never bend your head.

Always hold it high.

Look the world

Right in the eye.

~ Helen Keller

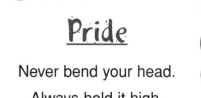

Responsibility

Y ou show **responsibility** by doing what you agree or promise to do. It might be a task, such as a homework assignment, or a chore, such as feeding your gerbil.

When you are young, your parents and teachers will give you simple tasks like putting away toys or brushing your teeth without being asked. As you get older, you will be given more responsibility. You might be trusted to come home from a friend's house at a certain time or drive to the store for groceries.

It takes a lot of practice to grow up to be a responsible person. The easiest way to practice is by keeping your promises and doing what you know is right.

A parent is responsible for different things than a child or a teenager. Write three activities you are responsible for every day. Then write three things a parent is responsible for every day.

If you want your eggs hatched, sit on them yourself. ~ **Haitian Proverb**

Activity

Materials needed:
21 pennies or counters such as beans, rocks, or marbles
2 small containers labeled #1 and #2

Decide on a reward for successfully completing this activity.
Put all the counters in container #1.
Review the three activities you are responsible for every day.
Each night before you go to bed, put one counter for each completed activity into container #2. At the end of seven days count all the counters in container #2.
If you have 16 or more counters in container #2, you are on your way to becoming very responsible. Collect your reward.
My reward is_____.

Service/Helping

Service is **helping** another person or group of people without asking for any kind of reward or payment. These are some good things that happen when you do service:

1. You feel closer to the people in your community (neighborhood).
2. You feel pride in yourself when you see that you can help other people in need.
3. Your family feels proud of you.
4. You will make new friends as you help others.

An old saying goes, "Charity begins at home." This means that you don't have to do big, important-sounding things to help people. You can start in your own home and neighborhood.

Activity

Each day this week, do one act of service around your house. Don't ask for or take any kind of payment or reward. Be creative! Possible acts of service are:

1. Carry in the groceries, do the dishes, or fold the laundry.
2. Read aloud to a younger brother or sister.
3. Make breakfast or pack lunches.
4. Recycle newspapers and cans.
5. Clean the refrigerator or your room.

At the end of the week, think of a project to do with your family that will help your community. You could play musical instruments or sing at a nursing home, set up a lemonade stand and give the money you make to the Special Olympics, offer to play board games with children in the hospital, or pick some flowers and take them to a neighbor. The list goes on and on.

All the flowers of tomorrow are in the seeds of today.
~ Indian Proverb

Word Find

Find these words that also mean *service*.

Word Bank		
help	assist	aid
charity	support	boost
benefit	contribute	guide

```
m v l a o d w f d r
c o n t r i b u t e
t b s x c a z v x q
s g p q g w b n y t
i v l y g u v x z i
s n e t e x m n m f
s f h d u d g t e e
a u c h a r i t y n
s u p p o r t u x e
b o o s t g f j g b
```

Honesty and Trust

Being an **honest** person means you don't steal, cheat, or tell lies. **Trust** is when you believe someone will be honest. If you are dishonest, or not truthful, people will not trust you.

You want to tell the truth because it is important to have your family and friends trust you. However, it takes courage to tell the truth, especially if you don't want people to get mad at you or be disappointed in the way you behaved.

How would your parents feel if you lied to them? People almost always find out about lies, and most parents will be more angry about a lie than if you had told them the truth in the first place.

When family or friends ask about something, remember that honesty is telling the truth. Honesty is telling what really happened. Honesty is keeping your promises. *Be proud of being an honest person.*

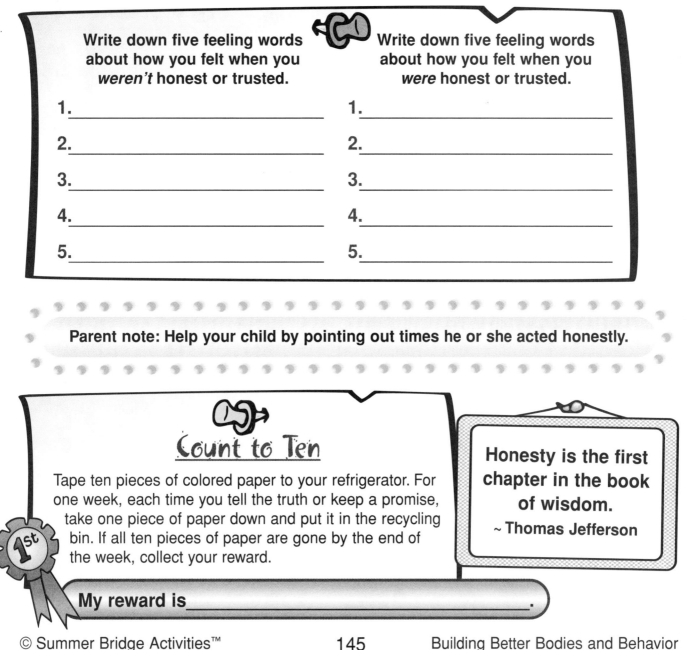

Write down five feeling words about how you felt when you *weren't* honest or trusted.

1. _____
2. _____
3. _____
4. _____
5. _____

Write down five feeling words about how you felt when you *were* honest or trusted.

1. _____
2. _____
3. _____
4. _____
5. _____

Parent note: Help your child by pointing out times he or she acted honestly.

Count to Ten

Tape ten pieces of colored paper to your refrigerator. For one week, each time you tell the truth or keep a promise, take one piece of paper down and put it in the recycling bin. If all ten pieces of paper are gone by the end of the week, collect your reward.

Honesty is the first chapter in the book of wisdom.

~ Thomas Jefferson

My reward is _____.

Happiness

Happiness is a feeling that comes when you enjoy your life. Different things make different people happy. Some people feel happy when they are playing soccer. Other people feel happy when they are playing the cello. It is important to understand what makes you happy so you can include some of these things in your daily plan.

These are some actions that show you are happy: laughing, giggling, skipping, smiling, and hugging.

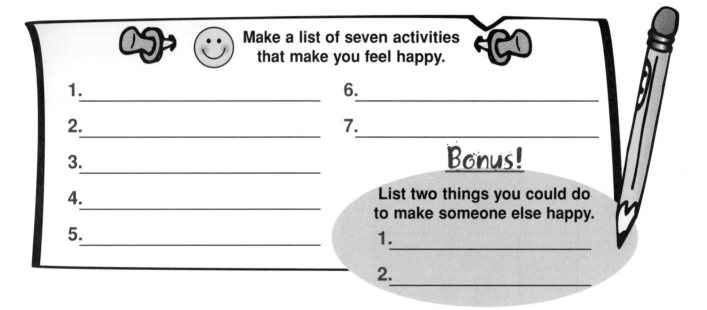

Make a list of seven activities that make you feel happy.

1._____
2._____
3._____
4._____
5._____

6._____
7._____

Bonus!

List two things you could do to make someone else happy.

1._____
2._____

Activity

Write down a plan to do one activity each day this week that makes you happy.

Try simple things—listen to your favorite song, play with a friend, bake muffins, shoot hoops, etc.

Be sure to thank everyone who helps you and don't forget to laugh!

Happy Thought

The world is so full

of a number of things,

I'm sure we should

all be happy as kings.

~Robert Louis Stevenson

Notes

_____
_____
_____
_____
_____
_____
_____
_____
_____
_____
_____
_____
_____
_____
_____
_____
_____
_____
_____

5 Five things I'm thankful for:

1. _____
2. _____
3. _____
4. _____
5. _____

Notes

_____

_____

_____

_____

_____

_____

_____

_____

_____

_____

_____

_____

_____

_____

_____

_____

_____

_____

_____

_____

_____

5 Five things I'm thankful for:

1. _____
2. _____
3. _____
4. _____
5. _____

Notes

_____
_____
_____
_____
_____
_____
_____
_____
_____
_____
_____
_____
_____
_____
_____
_____
_____
_____
_____
_____
_____
_____
_____

5 Five things I'm thankful for:

1. _____
2. _____
3. _____
4. _____
5. _____

Multiplication and Division

Developing multiplication and division math skills can be a challenging experience for both parent and child.

- **Have a positive attitude.**
- **Relax and enjoy the learning process.**
- **Keep the learning time short and fun you will get better results.**
- **Review the cards with your child.**
- **Read the front of the card.**
- **Check your answer on the reverse side.**
- **Separate those he/she does not know.**
- **Review those he/she does know.**
- **Gradually work through the other cards.**

These steps will help build your child's confidence with multiplication and division. Enjoy the rewards!

"Teacher, Teacher"

Three or more players.
Each player takes a turn as "Teacher."
The Teacher mixes up the flashcards and holds one card up at a time.
First player to yell out "Teacher, Teacher,"
will have the first chance to give the answer.
If his/her answer is right he/she receives 5 points.
If his/her answer is wrong, he/she will not receive any points.
Move on to the next person until someone answers correctly.
The next round someone else is teacher.
Repeat each round.
Reward the different levels, everyone wins!

Time Challenge

Follow the directions for "Teacher, Teacher" and add a time to it.
Increase the point system to meet the Time Challenge.
Reward the different levels, everyone wins!

0 x 0 4	0 x 1 3	0 x 2 2	0 x 3 1
0 x 4 8	0 x 5 7	0 x 6 6	0 x 7 5
0 x 8 3	0 x 9 2	0 x10 1	1 x 1 9

$1\overline{)1}$

0

$1\overline{)2}$

0

$1\overline{)3}$

0

$1\overline{)4}$

0

$1\overline{)5}$

0

$1\overline{)6}$

0

$1\overline{)7}$

0

$1\overline{)8}$

0

$1\overline{)9}$

1

$2\overline{)2}$

0

$2\overline{)4}$

0

$2\overline{)6}$

0

2	2	3	3
x 1	x 2	x 1	x 2
7	6	5	4

3	4	4	4
x 3	x 1	x 2	x 3
2	1	9	8

4	5	5	5
x 4	x 1	x 2	x 3
6	5	4	3

$2\overline{)8}$

6

$2\overline{)10}$

3

$2\overline{)12}$

4

$2\overline{)14}$

2

$2\overline{)16}$

12

$2\overline{)18}$

8

$3\overline{)3}$

4

$3\overline{)6}$

9

$3\overline{)9}$

15

$3\overline{)12}$

10

$3\overline{)15}$

5

$3\overline{)18}$

16

5 x 4 1	5 x 5 q	6 x 1 8	6 x 2 7
6 x 3 5	6 x 4 4	6 x 5 3	6 x 6 2
7 x 1 q	7 x 2 8	7 x 3 7	7 x 4 6

$3\overline{)21}$	$3\overline{)24}$	$3\overline{)27}$	$4\overline{)4}$
12	6	25	20
$4\overline{)8}$	$4\overline{)12}$	$4\overline{)16}$	$4\overline{)20}$
36	30	24	18
$4\overline{)24}$	$4\overline{)28}$	$4\overline{)32}$	$4\overline{)36}$
28	21	14	7

7 x 5	7 x 6	7 x 7	8 x 1
4	3	2	1
8 x 2	8 x 3	8 x 4	8 x 5
8	7	6	5
8 x 6	8 x 7	8 x 8	9 x 1
3	2	1	9

$5\overline{)5}$	$5\overline{)10}$	$5\overline{)15}$	$5\overline{)20}$
8	49	42	35

$5\overline{)25}$	$5\overline{)30}$	$5\overline{)35}$	$5\overline{)40}$
40	32	24	16

$5\overline{)45}$	$6\overline{)6}$	$6\overline{)12}$	$6\overline{)18}$
9	64	56	48

9 x 2 7	9 x 3 6	9 x 4 5	9 x 5 4
9 x 6 2	9 x 7 1	9 x 8 9	9 x 9 8
10 x 1 6	10 x 2 5	10 x 3 4	10 x 4 3

$6\overline{)24}$

45

$6\overline{)30}$

36

$6\overline{)36}$

27

$6\overline{)42}$

18

$6\overline{)48}$

81

$6\overline{)54}$

72

$7\overline{)7}$

63

$7\overline{)14}$

54

$7\overline{)21}$

40

$7\overline{)28}$

30

$7\overline{)35}$

20

$7\overline{)42}$

10

10 x 5	10 x 6	10 x 7	10 x 8
7	6	5	4
10 x 9	10 x 10	7)49	7)56
2	1	9	8
7)63	8)8	8)16	8)24
6	5	4	3

$8\overline{)32}$	$8\overline{)40}$	$8\overline{)48}$	$8\overline{)56}$
80	70	60	50

$8\overline{)64}$	$8\overline{)72}$	$9\overline{)9}$	$9\overline{)18}$
8	7	100	90

$9\overline{)27}$	$9\overline{)36}$	$9\overline{)45}$	$9\overline{)54}$
3	2	1	9

$9\overline{)63}$ 0

$9\overline{)72}$ 0

$9\overline{)81}$ 0

$10\overline{)10}$ 0

$10\overline{)20}$ 0

$10\overline{)30}$ 0

$10\overline{)40}$ 0

$10\overline{)50}$ 0

$10\overline{)60}$

$10\overline{)70}$

$10\overline{)80}$ 0

$10\overline{)90}$ 0

$1\overline{)0}$

$2\overline{)0}$

$3\overline{)0}$

$4\overline{)0}$

1

9

8

7

$5\overline{)0}$

$6\overline{)0}$

$7\overline{)0}$

$8\overline{)0}$

5

4

3

2

$9\overline{)0}$

$10\overline{)0}$

9

8

7

6

Certificate

of

Completion

Awarded to

_____

for the completion of Summer Bridge Activities™

3rd grade to 4th grade.

Ms. Hansen
Ms. Hansen

Mr. Fredrickson
Mr. Fredrickson

_____
Parent's Signature